THE
NO ASSHOLE
RULE

THE NO ASSHOLE RULE

Building a Civilized Workplace
and Surviving One That Isn't

ROBERT I. SUTTON, PhD

WARNER
BUSINESS
BOOKS ™

NEW YORK   BOSTON

Poem "Joe Heller" by Kurt Vonnegut reprinted by permission of author.

Warner Business Books
Hachette Book Group USA
1271 Avenue of the Americas
New York, NY 10020

Warner Business Books is an imprint of Warner Books.
Warner Business Books is a trademark of Time Warner Inc. or an affiliated company. Used under license by Hachette Book Group USA, which is not affiliated with Time Warner Inc.

Printed in the United States of America

ISBN-13: 978-0-7394-8725-9
Book design by Charles Sutherland

To Eve, Claire, and Tyler, with all my love

CONTENTS

THE
NO ASSHOLE
RULE

INTRODUCTION

When I encounter a mean-spirited person, the first thing I think is: "Wow, what an asshole!"

I bet you do, too. You might call such people bullies, creeps, jerks, weasels, tormentors, tyrants, serial slammers, despots, or unconstrained egomaniacs, but for me at least, *asshole* best captures the fear and loathing that I have for these nasty people.

I wrote this book because most of us, unfortunately, have to deal with assholes in our workplaces at one time or another. *The No Asshole Rule* shows how these destructive characters damage their fellow human beings and undermine organizational performance. This little book also shows how to keep these jerks out of your workplace, how to reform those you are stuck with, how to expel those who can't or won't change their ways, and how to best limit the destruction that these demeaning creeps cause.

I first heard of "the no asshole rule" more than fifteen years ago, during a faculty meeting at Stanford University.

Our small department was a remarkably supportive and collegial place to work, especially compared to the petty but relentless nastiness that pervades much of academic life. On that particular day, our chairman Warren Hausman was leading a discussion about who we ought to hire as a new faculty member.

One of my colleagues proposed that we hire a renowned researcher from another school, which provoked another to say, "Listen, I don't care if that guy won the Nobel Prize. . . . I just don't want any assholes ruining our group." We all had a good laugh, but then we started talking in earnest about how to keep demeaning and arrogant jerks out of our group. From that moment on, when discussing whether to hire faculty, it was legitimate for any of us to question the decision by asking: "The candidate seems smart, but would this hire violate our no asshole rule?" And it made the department a better place.

The language in other workplaces is more polite, including rules against being a "jerk," "weasel," or "bully." Other times, the rule is enforced but left unspoken. Whatever form the rule takes, a workplace that enforces "the no asshole rule" is where I want to be, not the thousands of organizations that ignore, forgive, or even encourage nastiness.

I didn't plan to write *The No Asshole Rule*. It all started in 2003 with a half-serious proposal that I made to *Harvard Business Review* when their senior editor Julia Kirby asked if I had any suggestions for *HBR*'s annual list of "Breakthrough Ideas." I told Julia that the best business practice

I knew of was "the no asshole rule," but *HBR* was too respectable, too distinguished, and quite frankly, too uptight to print that mild obscenity in their pages. I argued that censored and watered-down variations like "the no jerk rule" or "the no bully rule" simply didn't have the same ring of authenticity or emotional appeal, and I would be interested in writing an essay only if they actually printed the phrase "the no asshole rule."

I expected *HBR* to politely brush me aside. I secretly looked forward to complaining about the sanitized and naive view of organizational life presented in *HBR*'s pages—that their editors lacked the courage to print language that reflected how people actually think and talk.

I was wrong. *HBR* not only published the rule (under the headline "More Trouble Than They're Worth") in their "Breakthrough Ideas" section in February 2004, but the word *asshole* was printed a total of eight times in this short essay! After the article appeared, I received an even bigger surprise. Until this column, I had published four other *HBR* articles, and those pieces did generate some e-mail, phone calls, and press inquiries. But those reactions were trivial compared to the deluge provoked by the "no asshole" essay, even though it was buried among nineteen other "Breakthrough Ideas." I received dozens and dozens of e-mails in response to the "no asshole" essay (and a follow-up piece that I published in *CIO Insight*), and I still get more e-mail each month.

The first e-mail I got was from a manager at a roofing company who said that the essay inspired him to finally do something about a productive but abusive employee. Then messages started rolling in from people in all kinds of jobs from all around the world: an Italian journalist, a Spanish management consultant, an accountant at Towers-Perrin in Boston, a "minister counselor for management" at the U.S. Embassy in London, the manager of a luxury hotel in Shanghai, a benefits manager at a museum in Pittsburgh, the CEO of Mission Ridge Capital, a researcher at the United States Supreme Court, and on and on.

And while I expected my academic colleagues who study topics like bullying and aggression at work to find the term *asshole* too crude and too imprecise, many of them expressed support, including one who wrote, "Your work on the 'no asshole rule' has certainly resonated with my colleagues and me. In fact, we often speculate that we would be able to predict a large proportion of variance in job satisfaction with one 'flaming asshole item.' Basically, if we could ask whether [their] boss is one, we would not need any other [survey] items. . . . Thus, I agree that while potentially offensive, no other word quite captures the essence of this type of person."

My little *HBR* piece also generated press reports, stories, and interviews about the rule, at outlets including National Public Radio, *Fortune Small Business*, and my favorite, a column by Aric Press, editor in chief of the *American Lawyer*, who urged law firms to institute "jerk audits." Press proposed to firm leaders that "what I'm suggesting is that you ask yourselves this question: why do we put up with this behavior? If the answer is 2,500 value-billed hours, at least you will have identified your priorities without incurring the cost of a consultant."

Of course, lawyers and law firms are not unique. Nasty people are found in virtually every occupation and country; for instance, *arse*, *arsehole*, and more politely, *a nasty piece of work* are commonly uttered in the United Kingdom and would fit our inventory of *asshole* synonyms. The term *asshat* is a slightly less crude variation that is popular in online communities. *Assclown* is a version that was popularized by World Wrestling Entertainment star Chris Jericho and *The Office*, the hit British (and now American) television series about an idiotic and oppressive boss. Whatever these creeps are called, many of them are clueless about their behavior. Even worse, some of them are proud of it. Other jerks are troubled and embarrassed by their behavior, but can't seem to contain or control their meanness. All are similar, however, in that they infuriate, demean, and damage their peers, superiors, underlings, and at times, clients and customers, too.

I was convinced to write *The No Asshole Rule* by the fear and despair that people expressed to me, the tricks they used to survive with dignity in asshole-infested places, the revenge stories that made me laugh out loud, and the other small wins that they celebrated against mean-spirited people. I also wrote *The No Asshole Rule* because there is so much evidence that civilized workplaces are not a naive dream, that they do exist, and that pervasive contempt can be erased and replaced with mutual respect when a team or organization is managed right—and civilized workplaces usually enjoy superior performance as well. I hope that this little book will resonate with and provide comfort to all of you who feel oppressed by the jerks that you work with, serve, or struggle to lead. I also hope that it will provide you with practical ideas for driving out and reforming nasty people or, when that isn't possible, help you limit the damage that these creeps do to you and to your workplace.

CHAPTER 1

What Workplace Assholes Do and Why You Know So Many

Who deserves to be branded as an asshole? Many of us use the term indiscriminately, applying it to anyone who annoys us, gets in our way, or happens to be enjoying greater success than us at the moment. But a precise definition is useful if you want to implement the no asshole rule. It can help you distinguish between those colleagues and customers you simply don't like from those who deserve the label. It can help you distinguish people who are having a bad day or a bad moment ("temporary assholes") from persistently nasty and destructive jerks ("certified assholes"). And a good definition can help you explain to others *why* your coworker, boss, or customer deserves the label—or come to grips with why others say you are an asshole (at least behind your back) and why you might have earned it.

Researchers such as Bennett Tepper who write about psychological abuse in the workplace define it as "the sustained display of hostile verbal and nonverbal behavior, excluding physical contact." That definition is useful as far as it goes. But it isn't detailed enough for understanding what assholes do and their effects on others. An experience I had as a young assistant professor is instructive for understanding how assholes are defined in this little book. When I arrived at Stanford as a twenty-nine-year-old researcher, I was an inexperienced, ineffective, and extremely nervous teacher. I got poor teaching evaluations in my first year on the job, and I deserved them. I worked to become more effective in the classroom and was delighted to win the best-teacher award in my department (by student vote) at the graduation ceremony at the end of my third year at Stanford.

But my delight lasted only minutes. It evaporated when a jealous colleague ran up to me immediately after the graduating students marched out and gave me a big hug. She secretly and expertly extracted every ounce of joy I was experiencing by whispering in my ear in a condescending tone (while sporting a broad smile for public consumption), "Well, Bob, now that you have satisfied the babies here on campus, perhaps you can settle down and do some real work."

This painful memory demonstrates the two tests that I use for spotting whether a person is acting like an asshole:

- **Test One:** After talking to the alleged asshole, does the "target" feel oppressed, humiliated, de-energized, or belittled by the person? In particular, does the target feel worse about him or herself?
- **Test Two:** Does the alleged asshole aim his or her venom at people who are *less powerful* rather than at those people who are more powerful?

I can assure you that after that interaction with my colleague—which lasted less than a minute—I felt worse about myself. I went from feeling the happiest I'd ever been about my work performance to worrying that my teaching award would be taken as a sign that I wasn't serious enough about research (the main standard used for evaluating Stanford professors). This episode also demonstrates that although some assholes do their damage through open rage and arrogance, it isn't always that way. People who loudly insult and belittle their underlings and rivals are easier to catch and discipline. Two-faced backstabbers like my colleague, those who have enough skill and emotional control to save their dirty work for moments when they can't get caught, are tougher to stop—even though they may do as much damage as a raging maniac.

There are many other actions—sociologists call them interaction moves or simply moves—that assholes use to demean and deflate their victims. I've listed twelve common moves, a dirty dozen, to illustrate the range of these subtle and not subtle behaviors used by assholes. I suspect that you can add many more moves that you've seen, been subjected to, or done to others. I hear and read about new mean-spirited moves nearly every day. Whether we are talking about personal insults, status slaps (quick moves that bat down social standing and pride), shaming or "status degradation" rituals, "jokes" that are insult delivery systems, or treating people as if they are invisible, these and hundreds of other moves are similar in that they can leave targets feeling attacked and diminished, even if only momentarily. These are the means that assholes use to do their dirty work.

THE DIRTY DOZEN

Common Everyday Actions That Assholes Use

1. Personal insults
2. Invading one's "personal territory"
3. Uninvited physical contact
4. Threats and intimidation, both verbal and nonverbal
5. "Sarcastic jokes" and "teasing" used as insult delivery systems
6. Withering e-mail flames
7. Status slaps intended to humiliate their victims
8. Public shaming or "status degradation" rituals
9. Rude interruptions
10. Two-faced attacks
11. Dirty looks
12. Treating people as if they are invisible

The not so sweet thing that my colleague whispered in my ear also helps demonstrate the difference between a temporary asshole and a certified asshole. It isn't fair to call someone a certified asshole based on a single episode like this one; we can only call the person a temporary asshole. So while I would describe the colleague in my story as being a temporary asshole, we would need more information before labeling her as a certified asshole. Nearly all of us act like assholes at times; I plead guilty to multiple offenses. I once became angry with a staff member who I (wrongly) believed was trying to take an office away from our group. I sent an insulting e-mail to her and a copy to her boss, other faculty members, and her subordinates. She told me, "You made me cry." I later apologized to her. And although I don't demean one person after another day in and day out, I was guilty of being a jerk during that episode. (If you have never acted like an asshole even once in your life, please contact me immediately. I want to know how you've accomplished this superhuman feat.)

It is far harder to qualify as a certified asshole: a person needs to display a persistent pattern, to have a history of episodes that end with one "target" after another feeling belittled, put down, humiliated, disrespected, oppressed, de-energized, and generally worse about themselves. Psychologists make the distinction between states (fleeting feelings, thoughts, and actions) and traits (enduring personality characteristics) by looking for consistency across places and times—if someone consistently takes actions that leave a trail of victims in their wake, they deserve to be branded as certified assholes.

We all have the potential to act like assholes under the wrong conditions, when we are placed under pressure or, especially, when our workplace encourages everyone—especially the "best" and "most powerful" people—to act that way. Although it is best to use the term sparingly, some people do deserve to be certified as assholes because they are consistently nasty across places and times. "Chainsaw" Al Dunlap is a well-known candidate. The former Sunbeam CEO who wrote the book *Mean Business*, Dunlap was notorious for the verbal abuse he heaped on employees. In John Byrne's book *Chainsaw*, a Sunbeam executive described Dunlap as "like a dog barking at you for hours. . . . He just yelled, ranted, and raved. He was condescending, belligerent, and disrespectful."

Another candidate is producer Scott Rudin, known as one of the nastiest Hollywood bosses. The *Wall Street Journal* estimated that he went through 250 personal assistants between 2000 and 2005; Rudin claimed his records show only 119 (but admitted this estimate excluded assistants who lasted less than two weeks). His ex-assistants told the *Journal* that Rudin routinely swore and hollered at them—one said he was fired for bringing Rudin the wrong breakfast muffin, which Mr. Rudin didn't recall but admitted was "entirely possible." The online magazine *Salon* quotes a former assistant who received a 6:30 A.M. phone call from Rudin asking him to remind Rudin to send flowers to Anjelica Huston for her birthday. At 11:00 that same morning, Rudin called her into his office and screamed, "You asshole! You forgot to remind me to get flowers for Anjelica Huston's birthday!" This former assistant added, "And as he slowly disappears behind his automatic closing door, the last thing I see is his finger, flipping me off."

Nor is such behavior confined to men. According to the *New York Times*, Linda Wachner, former CEO of Warnaco, was infamous for publicly demeaning employees for missing performance goals or "simply displeasing her." Chris Heyn, former president of Warnaco's Hathaway shirt division, told the *New York Times*, "When you did not make numbers, she would dress you down and make you feel knee-high, and it was terrifying." Other former employees reported that Wachner's attacks were often "personal rather than professional, and not infrequently laced with crude references to sex, race, or ethnicity."

Famous bosses aren't the only ones who persistently demean their underlings. Many of the e-mail messages I got after my *Harvard Business Review* essay were tales about bosses who belittled and insulted their underlings day after day. Take the reader who wrote from Scotland, "A woman I know had a horrible boss. It was a very small office and didn't even have a toilet. She became pregnant and consequently needed the loo a lot. Not only would she have to go to a neighbouring shop, but the boss felt that the visits were too frequent and started counting them as her break time/lunchtime!" A former secretary at a large public utility told me that she quit her job because her (female) boss wouldn't stop touching her shoulders and her hair.

Take this excerpt from *Brutal Bosses and Their Prey* of an interview that Harvey Hornstein did with one victim of multiple humiliations:

"Billy," he said, standing in the doorway so that everyone in the central area could see and hear us clearly. "Billy, this is not adequate, really not at all." . . . As he spoke, he crumpled the papers that he held. My work. One by one he crumpled the papers, holding them out as if they were something dirty and dropping them inside my office as everyone watched. Then he said loudly, "Garbage in, garbage out." I started to speak, but he cut me off. "You give me the garbage; now you clean it up." I did. Through the doorway I could see people looking away because they were embarrassed for me. They didn't want to see what was in front of them: a thirty-six-year-old man in a three-piece suit stooping before his boss to pick up crumpled pieces of paper.

If these stories are accurate, all these bosses deserved to be certified as assholes because they were consistently nasty to the people they worked with, especially their underlings. This brings us to test two: Does the alleged asshole aim his or her venom at people who are *less powerful* rather than at those people who are more powerful? My colleague's behavior at the Stanford graduation ceremony qualifies because, when the episode occurred, this person was more senior and more powerful than I was.

This notion that the way a higher-status person treats a

lower-status person is a good test of character isn't just my idea. A test reflecting the same spirit was used by Sir Richard Branson, founder of the Virgin empire, to screen candidates for a reality television series where he selected "billionaires in the rough." *The Rebel Billionaire* was meant to compete with Donald Trump's wildly successful show *The Apprentice*. During the first episode, Branson picked up contestants at the airport while he was disguised as an arthritic old driver—then he kicked two of them off the show for treating him so badly when they believed he was an "irrelevant" human being.

Again, there is a difference between isolated incidents where people act like assholes versus people who are certified assholes—who consistently aim their venom at less powerful people and rarely, if ever, at more powerful people. John R. Bolton, the controversial U.S. ambassador to the United Nations, meets the test if the testimony to the U.S. Congress is correct. President George W. Bush made the controversial decision to appoint Bolton when he was on the verge of failing to be confirmed by Congress. Bolton's reputation for dishing out psychological abuse to colleagues fueled the media frenzy surrounding his appointment. Melody Townsel, for example, testified that she experienced Bolton's nastiness when she worked as a contractor for the U.S. Agency for International Development in Moscow in 1994. Townsel reported that Bolton turned mean after she complained about the incompetence of a client that Bolton (a lawyer) represented.

In Townsel's 2005 letter to the Senate Foreign Relations

Committee, she claimed that "Mr. Bolton proceeded to chase me through the halls of a Russian hotel—throwing things at me, shoving threatening letters under my door, and generally, behaving like a madman" and that "for nearly two weeks, while I awaited fresh direction . . . John Bolton hounded me in such an appalling way that I eventually retreated to my hotel room and stayed there. Mr. Bolton, of course, then routinely visited me there to pound on the door and shout threats." Townsel added, "He made unconscionable comments about my weight, my wardrobe, and with a couple of team leaders, my sexuality."

In other testimony to the committee, former Bolton subordinate Carl Ford Jr. (a fellow Republican) described him as a "kiss-up, kick-down sort of guy." In my opinion, if these reports are true, they indicate that Bolton qualifies as a certified asshole because his abuse is part of a persistent pattern, not just something out of character that happened once or twice because he was having a bad day.

I am not alone in this view. The *Village Voice* published an article titled "Wanted: Complete Asshole for U.N. Ambassador," which concluded that "John Bolton has left a trail of alienated colleagues and ridiculed ideas."

Don't Replace Assholes with Wimps and Polite Clones

It is also important to define the term *asshole* because this book is *not* an argument for recruiting and breeding spineless wimps. My focus is squarely on screening, reforming, and getting rid of people who demean and damage others, especially others with relatively little power. If you want to learn about the virtues of speaking quietly and the nuances of workplace etiquette, then read something by Miss Manners. I am a firm believer in the virtues of conflict, even noisy arguments. Research on everything from student groups to top management teams reveals that constructive arguments over ideas—but not nasty personal arguments— drives greater performance, especially when teams do nonroutine work. And, as I show in my book *Weird Ideas That Work*, organizations that are too narrow and rigid about whom they let in the door stifle creativity and become dreary places populated by dull clones.

The right kind of friction can help any organization. To take a famous example, Intel cofounder and retired CEO Andy Grove can be a strong-willed and argumentative person. But Grove is renowned for sticking to the facts and for inviting anyone—from brand-new Intel engineers to Stanford students whom he teaches about business strategy to senior Intel executives—to challenge his ideas. For Grove, the focus has always been on finding the truth, not on putting people down. Not only do I despise spineless and obsequious wimps, but there is good evidence that they damage organizations. A series of controlled experiments and field studies in organizations shows that when teams engage in conflict over ideas in an atmosphere of mutual respect, they develop better ideas and perform better. That is why Intel teaches employees how to fight, requiring all new hires to take classes in "constructive confrontation." These same studies show, however, that when team members engage in personal conflict—when they fight out of spite and anger—their creativity, performance, and job satisfaction plummet. In other words, when people act like a bunch of assholes, the whole group suffers.

I also want to put in a good word for socially awkward people, some of whom—through no fault of their own—are so socially insensitive that they accidentally act like assholes at times. Certainly, people with high emotional intelligence who are skilled at taking the perspectives of people they encounter and at responding to their needs and feelings are pleasant to be around and well suited for leadership positions. Yet many extremely valuable employees—as a result of everything from being raised in dysfunctional families to having disabilities like Asperger's syndrome, nonverbal learning disorders, and Tourette's syndrome—act strangely, have poor social skills, and inadvertently hurt other people's feelings.

A few years back, I wrote a book on building creative organizations called *Weird Ideas That Work*. As I did the research, I was struck by how many successful leaders of high-tech companies and creative organizations like advertising agencies, graphic design firms, and Hollywood production companies had learned to ignore job candidates' quirks and strange mannerisms, to downplay socially inappropriate remarks, and instead, to focus on what the people could actually do. I first heard this argument from Nolan Bushnell—the founder of Atari, which was the first wildly successful computer gaming company. Bushnell told me that although he looked for smooth-talking marketing people, when it came to technical people, he just wanted to see their work because "the best engineers sometimes come in bodies that can't talk." Later, I even learned that film students at places like the University of Southern California believe that "talent"—especially script writers—who come off as a bit strange are seen as more creative, so they consciously develop strange mannerisms and dress in odd ways, a process they call "working on your quirk."

The Evidence Fits Your Experience: Workplaces Have *a Lot* of Assholes

I don't know of any scholarly studies with titles like "the prevalence of assholes in the modern organization" or "interpersonal moves by assholes in the workplace: form and frequency." Most researchers are too dignified to use this dirty word in print. But I do know that each of my friends and acquaintances reports working with at least one "asshole." And when people hear that I am writing about the topic, I don't have to ask for stories about these jerks—the targets seek me out and tell me one asshole story after another.

This flood of anguished and amusing anecdotes may reflect my particular idiosyncrasies. I suspect that I am more easily offended by personal slights than most people, especially by people who are rude, nasty, or detached during service encounters. I am also married to a lawyer, an occupation that is rightly reputed to have more than its share of overbearing assholes. And because I have had a long-standing interest in the topic, I look for information about nasty people and remember it better than, say, about Good Samaritans, famous athletes, or unusually smart people.

There is also a big pile of scholarly research that reaches much the same conclusion without using the term "asshole." It is conducted under banners including bullying, interpersonal aggression, emotional abuse, abusive supervision, petty tyranny, and incivility in the workplace. These studies show that many workplaces are plagued by "interpersonal moves" that leave people feeling threatened and demeaned, which are often directed by more powerful people at less powerful people.

Consider some findings:

- A 2000 study by Loraleigh Keashly and Karen Jagatic found that 27% of workers in a representative sample of seven hundred Michigan residents experienced mistreatment by someone in the workplace, with approximately one out of six reporting persistent psychological abuse.
- In a 2002 study of workplace aggression and bullying in the U.S. Department of Veterans Affairs, Keashly and Joel Neuman surveyed nearly five thousand employees about exposure to sixty "negative workplace behaviors"; 36% reported "persistent hostility" from coworkers and supervisors, which meant "experiencing at least one aggressive behavior at least weekly for a period of a year." Nearly 20% of

employees in the sample reported being bothered "moderately" to "a great deal" by abusive and aggressive behaviors, including yelling, temper tantrums, put-downs, glaring, exclusion, nasty gossip, and (on relatively rare occasions) "pushing, shoving, biting, kicking, and other sexual and nonsexual assaults."

- Studies of nurses suggest that they are demeaned at an especially high rate. A 1997 study of 130 U.S. nurses published in the *Journal of Professional Nursing* found that 90% reported being victims of verbal abuse by physicians during the past year; the average respondent reported six to twelve incidents of abusive anger, being ignored, and being treated in a condescending fashion. Similarly, a 2003 study of 461 nurses published in *Orthopaedic Nursing* found that in the past month 91% had experienced verbal abuse—defined as mistreatment that left them feeling attacked, devalued, or humiliated. Physicians were the most frequent source of such nastiness, but it also came from patients and their families, fellow nurses, and supervisors.

When I was a graduate student at the University of Michigan, Daniel Denison and I spent a week interviewing and observing a team of surgical nurses, and we were appalled by how openly rude and downright abusive the male doctors were to the (largely) female nurses. Take the surgeon that we dubbed "Dr. Gooser" after we saw him chasing a female nurse down the hall while trying to pinch her behind. The nurses we interviewed bitterly complained that it was useless to report him to administrators because they would be labeled as troublemakers and be told "he is just joking." All they could do was avoid him as much as possible.

Christine Pearson and her colleagues have done extensive research on workplace incivility, a milder form of nastiness than emotional abuse or bullying. Their survey of 800 employees found that 10% witnessed daily incivility on their jobs and 20% were direct targets of incivility at least once a week. Pearson and her colleagues did another study of workplace incivility among 126 Canadian white-collar workers, which found that approximately 25% witnessed incivility of some kind on the job every day and 50% reported being direct targets of incivility at least once a week.

Researchers in Europe are partial to the term *bullying* rather than *psychological abuse*. Charlotte Rayner and her colleagues reviewed studies of bullying in British workplaces, and estimated that 30% of British workers experience encounters with bullies on at least a weekly basis. A British study of more than five thousand private- and public-sector employees found that about 10% had been bullied in the prior six months, and that about 25% had been victims and nearly 50% had witnessed bullying in the past five years. Studies in the United Kingdom find that the highest rates of workplace bullying happen to workers in prisons, schools, and the postal system but also reveal high rates in a sample of 594 "junior physicians" (similar to residents in the United States): 37% reported being bullied in the prior year, and 84% indicated they had witnessed bullying that was aimed at fellow junior physicians.

A host of other studies show that psychological abuse and bullying are common in other countries, including Austria, Australia, Canada, Germany, Finland, France, Ireland, and South Africa. A representative sample of Australian employees, for example, found that 35% reported being verbally abused by at least one coworker and 31% reported being verbally abused by at least one superior. A focused study of "nasty teasing" in a representative sample of nearly 5,000 Danish employees found that more than 6% were consistently exposed to this specific brand of workplace bullying. In the Third European Survey on Working Conditions, which was based on 21,500 face-to-face interviews with employees from countries of the European Union, 9% reported that they were exposed to persistent intimidation and bullying.

Much of this nastiness is directed by superiors to their subordinates (estimates run from 50% to 80%), with somewhat less between coworkers of roughly the same rank (estimates run from 20% to 50%), and "upward" nastiness—where underlings take on their superiors—occurs in less than 1% of cases. Findings about the proportion of men versus women involved in this nastiness are mixed, although it is clear that men and women are victimized at roughly the same rate. And it is especially clear that the lion's share of bullying and psychological abuse is within gender, with men more likely to bully men and women more likely to bully women. A Web-based survey by the Workplace Bullying & Trauma Institute, for example, found that 63% of women were victims of another woman, and 62% of men were victims of another man.

The question of whether bullying and abuse tend to be done more often by men or women remains unclear, with some of the best U.S. studies (including Keashly and Jagatic's representative study of Michigan employees) showing no discernable differences between the sexes, while European studies suggest that abusers are more likely to be men. European studies also show that it is common for a victim to be "mobbed" by multiple people, typically both men and women. In short, the stereotypical jerk might be a man, but there are also huge numbers of women in every country studied who demean, belittle, and de-energize their peers and underlings.

The list of academic writings on bullying, psychological abuse, mobbing, tyrants, and incivility in the workplace goes on and on—hundreds of articles and chapters have been published. Estimates of who is doing what to whom depend on the population studied and how the particular type of workplace abuse is defined and measured. But the evidence is ironclad: there are a lot of assholes out there.

The Best Measure of Human Character

Diego Rodriguez works at IDEO, a small innovation company I've studied and worked with for more than a decade. You will hear more about IDEO in this book because it is such a civilized place to work. Diego urges organizations to develop "a shock-proof, bullet-resistant asshole detector."

This chapter proposes two steps for detecting assholes: first, identify people who persistently leave others feeling demeaned and de-energized; second, look to see if their victims usually have less power and social standing than their tormentors.

These tests imply an even more fundamental lesson that runs through this book: *the difference between how a person treats the powerless versus the powerful is as good a measure of human character as I know.* I described how Richard Branson devised such a test to help him decide which wannabe billionaires to fire and which to keep on his TV show. I've seen much the same thing on a smaller scale at Stanford, albeit accidentally. Several years back, I encountered a perfect illustration of a senior faculty member who met this asshole test. Approached for help by a Stanford undergraduate, he at first brushed aside and refused to assist this student, who was trapped in bureaucratic red tape. But once this uppity faculty member learned that the student's parents were powerful executives and had donated generously to the university, he was instantly transformed into a helpful and charming human being.

To me, when a person is persistently warm and civilized toward people who are of unknown or lower status, it means that he or she is a decent human being—as they say in Yiddish, a real "mensch," the opposite of a certified asshole. Small decencies not only make you feel better about yourself, they can have other rewards as well. The sweet lesson learned by a former student of mine, Canadian Rhodes Scholar Charles Galunic, is a case in point. Charlie is now a management professor at INSEAD business school in France and is one of the most thoughtful people I've ever met. Charlie told me a lovely story about something that happened at a cold and crowded train station in Kingston, Ontario, when he was traveling to Toronto for his Rhodes Scholarship interviews. He was sitting and waiting for the train when he noticed an older couple who were standing and waiting. Charlie being Charlie, he immediately offered the two his seat, which they were happy to take. The next day, Charlie met the couple at a reception in Toronto for the scholarship finalists, and it turned out that the husband was a member of the selection committee. Charlie isn't sure if this small decency helped him win the prestigious scholarship—but I like to think that it did.

I wrote this book to help people build organizations where menschs like Charlie are routinely hired and celebrated—and, to steal a phrase from Groucho Marx, create workplaces where time wounds all heels—or at least reforms or banishes these creeps.

CHAPTER 2

The Damage Done: Why Every Workplace Needs the Rule

Every organization needs the no asshole rule because mean-spirited people do massive damage to victims, bystanders who suffer the ripple effects, organizational performance, and themselves. The harm that victims suffer is most conspicuous; it was certainly the main theme in the often harrowing stories that people told me in response to my essays on the evils of assholes. Among the most troubling and articulate accounts was in an e-mail from a former researcher at the United States Supreme Court:

> I have been on the receiving end of an organization, the third branch of government, that permitted the polar opposite of the no asshole rule to thrive. You are correct [in that] there was no physical violence, no injuries visible to the eye, unless one looks deeper

into the reasons for facial pallor, increased heart rate, the number of doctor visits, or OTC medicinal purchases. However, long-term psychological scars at the personal and organizational level are most evident to those who wish to inquire and listen. I experienced them firsthand. . . . I observed and experienced abuse patterns at the highest levels of government.

Listen to victims and bystanders like this researcher who bear the brunt of these creeps. Talk to managers, employment lawyers, consultants, and corporate coaches who struggle with "asshole management" problems. Read academic research under banners including bullying, emotional abuse, petty tyranny, harassment, mobbing, interpersonal aggression, and "bad behavior" at work. The bad news is relentless—it adds up to an unnerving trail of evidence about the damage done by temporary and certified assholes. Consider some of the worst of the human and organizational wreckage.

Damage to Victims

The damage caused by demeaning and uninvited advances from lecherous bosses, coworkers, and clients is well documented. So is the harm inflicted on victims of racial and religious discrimination, who are often excluded, belittled, and treated as invisible. But there is also growing evidence that equal-opportunity assholes can inflict great harm on their targets. The vile effects of asshole behavior are confirmed by numerous studies in the United States, Europe (especially the United Kingdom), and, recently, Australia and Asia.

Bennett Tepper's research on abusive supervision, for example, examined a representative of 712 employees in a midwestern city. He found that many of these employees had bosses who used ridicule, put-downs, the silent treatment, and insults like "Tells me I'm incompetent" and "Tells me my thoughts or feelings are stupid." These demeaning acts drove people out of organizations and sapped the effectiveness of those who remained. A six-month follow-up found that employees with abusive supervisors quit their jobs at accelerated rates, and those still trapped in their jobs suffered from less work and life satisfaction, reduced commitment to employers, and heightened depression, anxiety, and burnout. Similar findings are uncovered in dozens of other studies, with victims reporting reduced job satisfaction and productivity, trouble concentrating at work, and mental and physical health problems including difficulty sleeping, anxiety, feelings of worthlessness, chronic fatigue, irritability, anger, and depression.

The effects of assholes are so devastating because they sap people of their energy and esteem mostly through the accumulated effects of small, demeaning acts, not so much through one or two dramatic episodes. Consider the office administrator who told me that his boss never raises her voice, but he "dies a little" during every meeting in her office because he is treated "like nothing." He described how she rarely looks him in the eye during conversations; instead, she looks past him at herself in the mirror behind where he usually sits, admiring herself, sometimes primping and preening, other times seeming to make small adjustments in her delivery and facial expressions to improve what she sees in the mirror. Stories of extreme public humiliation are more dramatic and easier to remember, but such tiny indignities take their toll as we travel though our days. The brief nasty stares; the teasing and jokes that are really camouflaged public shaming and insults; the people who treat us as invisible, who exclude us from minor and major gatherings—all those nasty little slices of organizational life—don't just hurt for a moment. They have cumulative effects on our mental health and our commitment to our bosses, peers, and organizations.

Assholes have devastating cumulative effects partly because nasty interactions have a far bigger impact on our moods than positive interactions—*five times the punch*, according to recent research. Andrew Miner, Theresa Glomb, and Charles Hulin did a clever study in which each of forty-one employees carried palm-size computers. Each completed a brief survey via the device at four random intervals throughout the workday, over a two- to three-week period. The device would alert the employee, a short survey would be presented on the screen, and the employee would have twenty minutes to report (among other things) if he or she had a recent interaction with a supervisor or a coworker, and whether it was positive or negative. Employees completed a checklist about their current mood, whether they were "blue," "contented," "happy," and so on. The employees had more positive than negative interactions; for example, about 30% of interactions with coworkers were positive and 10% were negative. But *negative interactions had a fivefold stronger effect on mood than positive interactions*—so nasty people pack a lot more wallop than their more civilized counterparts.

These findings help explain why demeaning acts are so devastating. It takes numerous encounters with positive people to offset the energy and happiness sapped by a single episode with one asshole.

Battered Bystanders

Assholes don't just damage the immediate targets of their abuse. Coworkers, family members, or friends who watch—or just hear about—these ugly incidents suffer ripple effects. Tepper found that employees with abusive supervisors faced greater conflict between work and family, agreeing with statements like "The demands of my work interfere with my home and family life." The secondhand suffering that underlies such dry survey responses is exposed in this e-mail that a distressed wife sent me:

> My husband is one of the senior people who reports directly to such a CEO jerk. We moved from the Midwest for this "opportunity." It is so bad. The senior

people just below him all huddle together in one another's offices trying to give one another support, but they're all very conscious of the fact that any one of them could decide to throw in the towel and then the stress would be redistributed on those who are left. The verbal abuse my husband describes is unbelievable, and I know he doesn't tell me the worst of it.

The ripple effects on witnesses and bystanders, even those who are not direct witnesses to the asshole in action, were described by the former researcher at the United States Supreme Court quoted earlier:

> The impact was devastating on individuals, even those who did not have contact with the abusers. Truthful renditions of interactions created a mythical but real monster (and later monsters) that everyone feared. The impact on the organization and its capacity to respond to internal and external needs was equally damaging. Mistrust was palpable and rampant. Communication was reduced to CYA e-mail; long, detailed memos; and meetings with participant witnesses. Creative avoidance prompted increased use of after-hours voice mail, underground agreements among those who did trust one another, and liberal use of sick days.

European researchers have assembled the best evidence on ripple effects. As we saw in chapter 1, a British study of more than five thousand employees found that while 25% had been victims of bullying in the past five years, nearly 50% had witnessed bullying incidents. Another British study of more than seven hundred public-sector employees found that 73% of the witnesses to bullying incidents experienced increased stress and 44% worried about becoming targets themselves. A Norwegian study of more than two thousand employees from seven different occupational sectors found that 27% of employees claimed that bullying reduced their productivity, even though fewer than 10% reported being victims. The fear that bullies inject in the workplace appears to explain much of this additional damage; research in the United Kingdom found that more than one-third of witnesses wanted to intervene to help victims but were afraid to do so. Bullies drive witnesses and bystanders out of their jobs, just as they do to "firsthand" victims. Research summarized by Charlotte Rayner in the United Kingdom suggests that about 25% of bullied victims and about 20% of witnesses quit their jobs. So assholes don't just injure their immediate victims; their wicked ways can poison everyone in a workplace, including their own careers and reputations.

Assholes Suffer, Too

Demeaning jerks are victims of their own actions. They suffer career setbacks and, at times, humiliation. A hallmark of assholes is that they sap the energy from victims and bystanders. People who persistently leave others feeling de-energized undermine their own performance by turning coworkers and bosses against them and stifling motivation throughout their social networks.

The University of Virginia's Rob Cross and his colleagues asked people in three different organizational "networks"—strategy consultants, engineers, and statisticians—to rate each of their coworkers on the question "When you typically interact with this person, how does it affect your energy level?" Cross and his colleagues found that being an energizer was one of the strongest drivers for positive performance evaluations. The strategy consultants were especially prone to giving lower evaluations to the de-energizers in their ranks. The lesson is that if you sap the energy out of people, you may be sucking the life out of your career, too.

Assholes also suffer because even when they do their jobs well by other standards, they get fired. The high-ranking government official who did so much damage to the Supreme Court researcher and his colleagues was ultimately "retired" from her job. Despite his winning record and many fans, Indiana Hoosiers coach Bob Knight was finally fired for losing his temper one time too many. Yes, there are times when acting like an asshole has advantages; I consider these upsides in chapter 6. Yet on the whole, acting like an insensitive creep undermines rather than boosts your performance as well as your reputation. The best evidence is that jerks succeed despite rather than because of their nasty ways.

There can also be deep humiliation for assholes who are "outed." After Linda Wachner was fired as CEO of the financially troubled Warnaco in 2001, I suspect that she was hurt and embarrassed by a long story in the *New York Times* that listed one indignity after another that she allegedly heaped upon people in her path. The *Times* reported that she routinely made ethnic and racial slurs. Business partner Calvin Klein claimed, "She is abusive to our people. Verbally, the language is disgusting." Several former underlings reported that one "common practice" Wachner used was to make late-night phone calls to employees who had fallen out of favor and insist that they come to her office for a meeting early the next morning, and "then she would leave them sitting in a room for hours, sometimes the entire day, waiting for her." Reading stories like these about yourself in one of the most widely circulated newspapers in the world has to be painful, even if you are a certified asshole.

This stigma can tar ordinary people, not just the rich and famous. Consider a lawyer named Richard Phillips at Baker & McKenzie's London office. He kept hounding a secretary named Jenny Amner to cough up about £4 (about $7) to pay for a ketchup stain on his trousers that she had accidentally caused. In an e-mail exchange between Phillips and Amner that spread on the Internet, she explained, "I must apologise for not getting back to you straight away, but due to my mother's sudden illness, death, and funeral, I have had more pressing issues than your £4. I apologise again for accidentally getting a few splashes of ketchup on your trousers. Obviously your financial need as a senior associate is greater than mine as a mere secretary."

Baker & McKenzie acknowledged, "We confirm we are aware of the incident and subsequent e-mail exchange. This is a private matter between two members of our staff that clearly got out of hand. We are investigating so as to resolve it as amicably as we can." Phillips resigned shortly after the incident. The *Daily Telegraph* reported that he was "devastated at his public humiliation," although Baker & McKenzie's spokesperson asserted that he had resigned well before the incident became public.

Impaired Organizational Performance

The damage that assholes do to their organizations is seen in the costs of increased turnover, absenteeism, decreased commitment to work, and the distraction and impaired individual performance documented in studies of psychological abuse, bullying, and mobbing. The effects of assholes on turnover are obvious and well documented. I don't feel sorry for him, but it must have cost Scott Rudin a fortune—and a lot of time—to manage the entrances and exits of the 119 assistants that worked for him between 2000 and 2005 (or 250 assistants, if you accept the *Wall Street Journal*'s estimate rather than Rudin's). And although Warnaco's general counsel described the turnover during Wachner's reign as "tracking" industry patterns, executive recruiters reported that it was the highest rate in the industry. Warnaco insiders told the *New York Times*, "Her personal criticism of employees, among other things, has led to excessive staff turnover and robbed the company of talent it needed to maintain quality operations." Under Wachner's leadership, Warnaco had "employed three chief financial officers at the Authentic Fitness division in five years, five presidents of Calvin Klein Kids in three years, and three heads of Warnaco Intimate Apparel in four years."

The question of whether it is against the law to be an equal-opportunity asshole, who belittles and demeans others in the workplace independently of gender, race, or religious beliefs, isn't yet resolved in the United States and other countries. But organizations that shelter assholes risk greater legal costs regardless of future court rulings—because claims made by victims of sexual harassment and discrimination are easier to prove when open hostility runs rampant. Attorney Paul Buchanan of Stoel Rives LLP wrote an essay for the Washington State Bar Association that asked, "Is it against the law to be a jerk?" He concluded that it probably isn't, at least for now. But Buchanan warned, "While the true equal-opportunity jerk usually is breaking no law, proving that the offending employee doled out abuse without discrimination may be a difficult and awkward task for an employer. Employers who fail to discipline aggressively and weed out (or at least train and reform) the boor, the bully, the power-monger, and even the person who simply lacks basic interpersonal skills may find themselves vulnerable to expensive and difficult employment lawsuits as disgruntled employees ascribe some unlawful motivation to the abusive conduct."

There are hints from outside the United States that judges and juries are starting to crack down on equal-opportunity assholes. Courts in the United Kingdom in particular are beginning to punish companies that allow bullying to persist, including a 2001 settlement against Mercury Mobile Communications Services for £370,000 (more than $600,000). Mercury allowed manager Simon Stone to conduct a "vendetta" of "open abuse and false accusations" against Jeffery Long, a procurement manager who had reported Stone's management failings to company directors. Long became physically ill, and his marriage dissolved as a result of the stress. Mercury ultimately admitted liability in court in addition to paying Long this large sum.

There are other insidious, but more subtle, ways that these bullies and jerks undermine performance. A hallmark of teams and organizations that are led by assholes, or where swarms of assholes run rampant, is that they are riddled with fear, loathing, and retaliation. In a fear-based organization, employees constantly look over their shoulders and constantly try to avoid the finger of blame and humiliation; even when they know how to help the organization, they are often afraid to do it. Consider research by Jody Hoffer Gittell on the airline industry published in the *California Management Review*. I was struck by her description of how American Airlines handled delayed planes and other performance problems in the 1990s. American's employees told Gittell that the fear of then-CEO Robert Crandall drove people to point fingers at one another rather than to fix problems. Crandall justified his approach by saying, "The last thing most of them want is the spotlight on them. I just increased the amount they have to do to keep the spotlight off themselves." Although some insiders admired Crandall's ability to uncover the "root cause" of delays, Gittell concluded that his tough approach backfired because many employees were so afraid of Crandall's wrath that they devoted their energy to protecting themselves, not to helping the company. One field manager told Gittell that when there was a delay, "Crandall wants to see the corpse. . . . It is management by intimidation." People focused on protecting themselves from "recrimination" rather than on "on-time performance, accurate baggage handling, and customer satisfaction."

A similar theme emerges from research by Amy Edmondson on nurses who have intimidating supervisors and unsupportive colleagues (or, as I would put it, people who are knee-deep in assholes). Edmondson did what she thought was a straightforward study of how leadership and coworker relationships influenced drug-treatment errors in eight nursing units. She assumed that the better the leadership and coworker support, the fewer mistakes people would make.

Yet Edmondson, along with the Harvard Medical School physicians funding her research, were at first bewildered when questionnaires showed that units with the *best* leadership and coworker relationships reported the *most* errors: *units with the best leaders reported making as many as ten times more errors than the units with the worst leaders.* After Edmondson pieced together all the evidence, she figured out that nurses in the best units reported far more errors because they felt "psychologically safe" to admit their mistakes. Nurses in the best units said that "mistakes were natural and normal to document" and that "mistakes are serious because of the toxicity of the drugs, so you are never afraid to tell the nurse manager."

The story was completely different in the units where nurses rarely reported errors. Fear ran rampant. Nurses said things like "The environment is unforgiving; heads will roll," "you get put on trial," and that the nurse manager "treats you as guilty if you make a mistake" and "treats you like a two-year-old." As the late corporate quality guru W. Edwards Deming concluded long ago, when fear rears its ugly head, people focus on protecting themselves, not on helping their organizations improve. Edmondson's research shows that this happens even when lives are at stake.

The loathing and dissatisfaction that assholes provoke also has costs in addition to increased turnover. Tepper's research showed that abusive supervisors dampen commitment to the organization. Other researchers have shown repeatedly that when people feel mistreated and dissatisfied with their jobs, they are unwilling to do extra work to help their organizations, to expend "discretionary effort." But when they feel supported and satisfied, the story is completely different.

In the late 1970s, industrial psychologist Frank J. Smith demonstrated the power of work attitudes on "discretionary effort" in a study of three thousand employees at Sears headquarters in Chicago. Smith found that employee attitudes didn't predict which employees were absent from work until the day a crippling snowstorm hit Chicago. On that day, when employees had a good excuse to stay home, employees who were more satisfied with their supervision and other parts of the job were far more likely to make the tough commute into work than those who were dissatisfied. Attendance in the twenty-seven employee groups that Smith studied averaged 70% (96% was typical) and ranged from 37% to 97%. Whether or not employees in a group were satisfied with their supervision was among the strongest predictors of attendance that snowy day. It makes sense to me. When I am stuck working for, or with, a bunch of assholes, I don't go out of my way to help. But when I admire my superiors and colleagues, I'll go to extreme lengths.

There is even evidence that when people work for cold and mean-spirited jerks, employees steal from their companies to even the score. Jerald Greenberg studied three nearly identical manufacturing plants in the midwestern United States; two of the three plants (which management chose at random) instituted a ten-week-long, 15% pay cut after the firm temporarily lost a major contract. In one plant where the cuts were implemented, an executive announced the cuts in a curt and impersonal manner and warned employees, "I'll answer one or two questions, but then I have to catch a plane for another meeting." In the second plant, the executive gave a detailed and compassionate explanation, along with sincere apologies for the cut and multiple expressions of remorse. The executive then spent a full hour answering questions. Greenberg found fascinating effects on employee theft rates. In the plant where no pay cuts were made, employee theft rates held steady at about 4% during the 10-week period. In the plant where the pay cut was done but explained in a compassionate way, the theft rate rose to 6%. And in the plant were the cuts were explained in a curt manner, the theft rate rose to nearly 10%.

After the pay levels were restored in the two plants, the theft rates returned to the same level (about 4%) as before the pay cuts were made. Greenberg believes that employees stole more in both plants where cuts were made to "get even" with their employer, but that they stole far more to exact revenge from the leader who was cold-hearted and "too busy" to provide an explanation.

We all know people shouldn't steal, and we all know that many people do steal. Greenberg's study, along with numerous controlled experiments, suggests that when people believe that they work for insensitive jerks, they find ways to get back at them, and stealing is one of those ways. Revenge isn't pretty, but it is a part of human nature that assholes bring out in their victims.

*   *   *

If word leaks out that your organization seems to be led by mean-spirited jerks, the damage to its reputation can drive away potential employees and shake investor confidence. Neal Patterson, CEO of the Cerner Corporation, learned this lesson in 2001 when he sent out a "belligerent" e-mail that was intended for just the top four hundred people in this health-care-software firm. According to the *New York Times*, Patterson complained that few employees were working full forty-hour weeks, and "as managers—you either do not know what your EMPLOYEES are doing; or you do not CARE." Patterson said that he wanted to see the employee parking lot "substantially full" between 7:30 A.M. and 6:30 P.M. on weekdays and "half full on Saturdays," and that if it didn't happen, he would take harsh measures, perhaps even layoffs and hiring freezes. Patterson warned, "You have two weeks. Tick, tock."

Patterson's e-mail was leaked onto the Internet, provoking harsh criticism from management experts, including my Stanford colleague Jeffrey Pfeffer, who described it as "the corporate equivalent of whips and ropes and chains." Jeff went a bit overboard for my tastes. But investors weren't pleased, either, as the value of the stock plummeted 22% in three days. Patterson handled the aftermath well. He sent an apology to his employees and admitted that he wished he had never sent the e-mail, and the share price did bounce back. Patterson learned the hard way that when CEOs come across as bullies, they can scare their investors, not just their underlings.

The Upshot: What Is Your Organization's "Total Cost of Assholes"?

A *Harvard Business Review* reader wrote me a lovely note suggesting that more companies would be convinced to enforce the rule if they estimated the "total cost of assholes," or their "TCA." As he put it, "The organizational impact, in terms of both retention and recruitment, lost clients, [and] excess organizational calories being expended on the wrong things could provide some very interesting insights."

Calculating the exact TCA for any organization is an unrealistic goal; there are just too many different factors and too much uncertainty. It is impossible, for example, to estimate exactly how many hours that managers devote to "asshole management" or to predicting future legal costs incurred by assholes in any organization. Yet going through the exercise of calculating your organization's TCA is still an instructive way to think about the costs of putting up with these bullies and bastards. As I scoured through pertinent research and talked to experienced managers and attorneys, I was stunned by the breadth and amount of these costs. In the list "What's Your TCA?" I present a series of factors, which includes those touched on in this chapter along with numerous others that I've encountered but haven't discussed. If you want to develop a rough estimate of your company's TCA, take a look at my long (but still incomplete) list of possible costs, attach the best cost estimate you can get to each one, and add any factors I've left out.

This exercise can help you come to terms with the damage that both temporary and certified assholes do to your organization, which is useful for convincing yourself and others to do something about this problem instead of tolerating it or talking about—but not actually implementing—any solutions. It is also useful for convincing yourself to stop belittling others and for getting some help if you can't stop yourself, as it can ruin not only others' lives, but also your own. Another reason for trying to attach dollar figures to these costs is that in the seemingly rational and numbers-driven business world, no matter how compelling your stories and lists of drawbacks might be, people from accounting, finance, and other quantitative backgrounds often rule the roost, and they seem to prefer to make decisions on the basis of bad (even useless) financial estimates rather than no estimates at all. So it might be wise to use the language they want to hear, no matter how rough the estimates.

Researchers Charlotte Rayner and Loraleigh Keashly demonstrate how to produce estimates of such costs. They start by estimating (based on past studies in the United Kingdom) that 25% of bullying "targets" and 20% of "witnesses" leave their jobs, and that the "average" bullying rate in the U.K. is 15%. Rayner and Keashly calculate that in an organization of one thousand people, if 25% of the bullied leave, and the replacement cost is $20,000, then the annual cost is $750,000. They add that if there is an average of two witnesses for each victim, and 20% leave, that adds $1.2 million, for a total replacement cost just shy of $2 million per year.

Rayner and Keashly use assumptions that will vary wildly from place to place, so it is instructive to look at the costs that one company estimated were inflicted by one asshole in one year. When I told a senior executive from a Silicon Valley company about the "total cost of assholes" concept, he said, "It is more than a concept; we just calculated it for one of our people." He told me that one of their most highly compensated salespeople—let's call him Ethan—was consistently ranked in their top 5% of producers. Ethan qualifies as a certified asshole: his temper is legendary; he treats his coworkers as rivals, routinely insulting and belittling them; his nasty late-night e-mail rants are infamous; and, not surprisingly, many insiders refuse to work with him. His last assistant lasted less than a year. No other assistant in the company was willing to work for Ethan, so they were forced to start a long and expensive search for a replacement. After all, finding someone who had even a slim chance of working successfully with Ethan was a tall order. Meanwhile, HR managers and, at times, senior executives were spending huge chunks of time running interference between Ethan and the company's support network. In the prior five years, several colleagues and administrative assistants had lodged "hostile workplace" complaints against Ethan. The company also spent a substantial amount of money on Ethan's anger management classes and counseling.

The company decided that in addition to warnings and training, it was time to quantify the incremental costs of Ethan's bad behavior and deduct it from his bonus. They did a week-by-week calculation of the extra costs of Ethan's nasty and inconsiderate actions compared to other, more civilized salespeople. HR managers estimated that costs for the prior year—time and dollars spent related to Ethan's treatment of people—totaled about $160,000. I find these costs disturbing, as they reflect so much suffering and heartache, so much time wasted by talented people. The figure also almost certainly understates full financial damage, as it omits physical and mental health effects on victims, time lost by and the emotional and physical toll on witnesses and bystanders, and the negative effects of the fear, loathing, and dysfunctional competition he provoked. The estimated costs were:

- Time spent by Ethan's direct manager:
  250 hours   valued at $25,000
- Time spent by HR professionals:
  50 hours   valued at $5,000
- Time spent by senior executives:
  15 hours   valued at $10,000
- Time spent by the company's outside
  employment counsel: 10 hours   valued at $5,000
- Cost of recruiting and training a new
  secretary to support Ethan $85,000

- Overtime costs associated with Ethan's
  last-minute demands $25,000
- Anger management training and
  counseling $5,000

Estimated total cost of asshole for one year   **$160,000**

An executive and an HR manager met with Ethan and reviewed these costs. They told him that the company would deduct 60% of the cost from what he otherwise would have earned as his year-end bonus. The reaction was predictable—Ethan flew into a rage and blamed the idiots he worked with for being unable to keep up with his expectations and requirements. He threatened to quit (but didn't). I applaud this company for calculating these costs, confronting Ethan with them, and insisting that he pay the price. If the executives were serious about enforcing a no asshole rule, however, they would have shown Ethan the door years ago—which is why I next turn to how to implement, enforce, and sustain a no asshole rule.

The bad news is that these oppressors cost organizations far more than their leaders and investors usually realize. The good news is that if you devote yourself and your organization to establishing and enforcing the no asshole rule, you can save a lot of money and save your people, their friends and families, and yourself *a lot* of heartache.

WHAT'S YOUR TCA?

*Factors to Consider When Calculating
the Total Cost of Assholes to Your Organization*

Damage to Victims and Witnesses

- Distraction from tasks—more effort devoted to avoiding nasty encounters, coping with them, and avoiding blame; less devoted to the task itself
- Reduced "psychological safety" and associated climate of fear undermines employee suggestions, risk taking, learning from own failures, learning from others' failures, and forthright discussion—honesty may not be the best policy
- Loss of motivation and energy at work
- Stress-induced psychological and physical illness
- Possible impaired mental ability
- Prolonged bullying turns victims into assholes
- Absenteeism
- Turnover in response to abusive supervision and peers—plus more time spent while at work looking for new work

Woes of Certified Assholes

- Victims and witnesses hesitate to help, cooperate with them, or give them bad news
- Retaliation from victims and witnesses
- Failure to reach potential in the organization
- Humiliation when "outed"
- Job loss
- Long-term career damage

Wicked Consequences for Management

- Time spent appeasing, calming, counseling, or disciplining assholes
- Time spent "cooling out" employees who are victimized
- Time spent "cooling out" victimized customers, contract employees, suppliers, and other key outsiders
- Time spent reorganizing departments and teams so that assholes do less damage
- Time spent interviewing, recruiting, and training replacements for departed assholes and their victims
- Management burnout, leading to decreased commitment and increased distress

Legal and HR Management Costs

- Anger management and other training to reform assholes
- Legal costs for inside and outside counsel
- Settlement fees and successful litigation by victims
- Settlement fees and successful litigation by alleged assholes (especially wrongful-termination claims)
- Compensation for internal and external consultants, executive coaches, and therapists
- Health-insurance costs

When Assholes Reign: Negative Effects on Organizations

- Impaired improvement in established systems
- Reduced innovation and creativity
- Reduced cooperation and cohesion
- Reduced "discretionary" effort
- Dysfunctional internal cooperation

- Costs of victims' retribution toward the organization
- Impaired cooperation from outside organizations and people
- Higher rates charged by outsiders—"combat pay" for working with assholes
- Impaired ability to attract the best and brightest

CHAPTER 3

How to Implement the Rule, Enforce It, and Keep It Alive

Many organizations enforce the no asshole rule, but some do it with a lot more zeal than others. In most places, certified assholes are *tolerated, but only up to a point.* People can get away with being run-of-the-mill jerks and might even score kudos and cash as a result. The rule is applied, but only to flaming assholes, who are punished, "reeducated," and then expelled if less drastic measures fail. The imaginary line between an ordinary and a flaming asshole depends on local quirks and customs. An "über-jerk" might be crowned after costing the organization a fortune, driving coworkers to the edge of madness, creating horrific PR problems, or exposing the organization to massive legal risk—even though hordes of ordinary jerks continue to get off scot-free.

This low standard was apparently applied to Ethan, the

abusive salesman whom I talked about in chapter 2. Management wasn't planning to fire this demeaning star, but they finally got fed up with his shenanigans and decided to document the costs and deduct them from his pay. But executives continued to take no action against a host of ordinary assholes at the company. Even organizations that seem to glorify arrogant jerks, like sports teams, can reach a breaking point where superstar coaches or players are so destructive that they are punished and kicked out.

Take what happened to legendary basketball coach Bob Knight at the University of Indiana. University president Myles Brand finally fired Knight in September 2000 after an incident with a student named Kent Harvey, who reportedly called out, "Hey, Knight, what's up?" as they walked past each other on campus. The student claimed that Knight roughly grabbed him by the arm and berated him for his poor manners. Knight argued that the student was exaggerating, but Brand announced that Knight was fired for a "pattern of unacceptable behavior," called Knight "defiant and hostile," and charged that the coach had demonstrated a "continued unwillingness" to work within the school's guidelines. Indiana administrators had tolerated Knight's antics for decades. He wasn't fired even after being accused of choking one of his players during a 1997 practice (a misdeed caught on a grainy videotape and shown by CNN/Sports Illustrated in March 2000). But university administrators finally got fed up with the damage that Knight was causing to Indiana's reputation with his outbursts, and they sent him packing.

More recently, in 2005, Philadelphia Eagle Terrell Owens paid the price for his relentless arrogance, bad-mouthing teammates (e.g., publicly blaming "tired" quarterback Donovan McNabb for Philadelphia's 2005 Super Bowl loss), and his apparent inability to control his rage (e.g., reports of a fight with team official Hugh Douglas). In late 2005, Eagles management finally suspended him for "conduct detrimental to the team" and made it clear that they didn't want him back. Owens defended himself by arguing that he was frustrated because he felt "disrespected" by his teammates.

People like Knight and Owens got away with so much for so long because, at least in the United States, we embrace clichés like "Winning isn't everything; it's the only thing" and "Second place means being the first loser." In fact, Knight was soon hired to coach the basketball team at Texas Tech University, and Owens was signed by the Dallas Cowboys for a reported $25 million contract, which included a $5 million signing bonus. As one executive and venture capitalist told me, the unspoken standard in American sports, business, medicine, and academia is: "The more often you are right and the more often you win, the bigger jerk you can be." He argued that in most places being an asshole is a disadvantage, that nastiness and outbursts are seen as character flaws—but are tolerated when people are more talented, smarter, more difficult to replace, and endowed with a higher natural success rate than ordinary mortals. "Extraordinary talent" is an all-purpose justification for tolerating, pampering, and kissing up to these destructive jerks. Our societal standard appears to be: *If you are a really big winner, you can get away with being a really big asshole.*

Yet it doesn't need to be that way. Some of the most effective and civilized organizations that I know disdain, punish, and drive out ordinary jerks and have no patience for them. As Shona Brown, Google's senior vice president for business operations, put it, the company acts on its "Don't be evil" motto by making Google a place *where it simply isn't efficient to act like an asshole.*

As Shona told me, yes, there are people at Google who might fit my definition of an asshole, but the company works to screen them out in hiring, and nasty people suffer during performance evaluations and aren't promoted to management positions. And Google has zero tolerance for what I call flaming assholes (Shona put it more politely, but that is what she meant).

Some companies take the rule even further. Ann Rhoades headed the "people department" at Southwest Airlines for years and was the founding head of human resources at JetBlue Airlines. Ann told me that at that both companies, it wasn't just inefficient to be a certified asshole; she said that employees couldn't get away with it, that "there is no place for them to hide." During the first year that JetBlue flew, Ann told me that "lack of cultural fit," especially having a bad attitude toward colleagues, customers, and the company, was the main "performance" reason that employees were fired. Southwest has always emphasized that people are "hired and fired for attitude."

Herb Kelleher, Southwest cofounder and former CEO, described how this works: "One of our pilot applicants was very nasty to one of our receptionists, and we immediately rejected him. You can't treat people that way and be the kind of leader we want." As Ann put it, "We don't do it to our people; they don't deserve it. People who work for us don't have to take the abuse."

At places that are most vehement and effective at enforcing the no asshole rule, "employee performance" and "treatment of others" aren't separate things. Phrases like "talented jerk," "brilliant bastard," or "an asshole and a superstar" are seen as oxymorons. Temporary assholes are dealt with immediately: they quickly realize (or are told) that they have blown it, apologize, reflect on their nastiness, ask for forgiveness, and work to change—rather than justify or glorify—their actions. Certified assholes aren't ignored or forgiven again and again; they change or are sent packing. At the places where I want to work, even if people do other things well (even extraordinary well) but routinely demean others, they are seen as incompetent.

Make It Public—by What You Say and *Especially* What You Do

Most organizations, especially big ones, have written policies that sound like censored versions of the no asshole rule. Many reinforce the message by posting it widely (usually with a list of other "core values") and teach it during employee orientation sessions. Senior managers routinely talk about the virtues of mutual respect or words to that effect. Some leaders and organizations even use the uncensored version of the rule.

As I mentioned in the opening pages, my colleagues and I talked openly about the rule in my academic department at Stanford. And several readers of my *Harvard Business Review* essay wrote to tell me that the rule was a centerpiece of their leadership style. My favorite was from Roderick C. Hare, CEO of Mission Ridge Capital: "For most of my professional career, I have been telling anyone who would listen that I can work with just about every type of person, with one glaring exception—assholes. In fact, I have always used that very word. As much as I believe in tolerance and fairness, I have never lost a wink of sleep about being unapologetically intolerant of anyone who refuses to show respect for those around them."

A few organizations talk about the rule as a centerpiece of their culture. A survey on Emplawyernet.com reported that McDermott Will & Emery, an international law firm with headquarters in Chicago, had a time-honored no asshole rule, which holds that "you're not allowed to yell at your secretary or yell at each other." McDermott's PR people emphasized to me that this is an informal rather than official policy, but they acknowledge that the firm's partners have talked about it for years. Or consider Success-Factors, a talent management software firm with headquarters in San Mateo, California. CEO Lars Dalgaard told me that a core company value is "respect for the individ-ual, no assholes—it's okay to have one, just don't be one." Dalgaard added that the rule was an "unequivoal message and all employees sign a contract committing to not being one," because "assholes stifle performance."

Similarly, the Canadian production company Apple Box Productions has since dissolved, but during the twelve years in which it cranked out one successful tele-vision commercial after another, the rule was a primary operating principle. Apple Box executive producer J.J. Lyons told trade magazines, "Internally and externally, we like to surround ourselves with nice people." He went on to say, "We have an internal rule here, sort of a motto; it's a thing called 'the no asshole rule.' If you're an asshole di-rector or producer, we don't want to work with you." His reason? "Life is too short." I say amen to that.

Most organizations express the rule in more polite lan-guage. At Plante & Moran, which was ranked twelfth on *Fortune* magazine's "100 Best Companies to Work For" list in 2006, "The goal is a 'jerk-free' workforce at this ac-counting firm" and "the staff is encouraged to live by the Golden Rule." In *BusinessWeek* Barclays Capital chief oper-ating officer Rich Ricci said that, especially in selecting senior executives, "we have a no jerk rule around here." *BusinessWeek* explained what this means: "Hotshots who alienate colleagues are told to change or leave." And at Xilinx, a semiconductor firm, "employees should respect and support each other even if they don't like each other." Or take the Men's Wearhouse, the most successful seller of men's suits in the United States, which has the most impressive and detailed philosophy I've ever seen. Consider a few of the company's values: "Everyone deserves to be treated fairly. If leaders are the problem, we ask those being served by leaders to let them know or go up the chain of command—without the threat of retaliation." "Store appearance and product knowledge are certainly important, but customer comfort and satisfaction during the shopping experience hinge on something else: our store team *must* feel emotionally energized and authentic in building service relationships with our customers." And most pertinent to the no asshole rule: "We respond immediately if any individual degrades another, regardless of position. In so doing, we demonstrate that we value all people."

As admirable as these sentiments are, posting them on a wall or Web site or talking about them are—alone—useless acts. And if these values are routinely violated and no steps are taken to enforce them, these hollow words are worse than useless. Jeff Pfeffer and I learned this lesson about hollow talk when writing *The Knowing-Doing Gap*, a book about why leaders and companies sometimes say smart things yet fail to do them and how to overcome this widespread malady. We call this impediment to action "the smart talk trap." To illustrate, a group of our students did a case study of a prominent securities firm, which had three values that top management talked about constantly and were displayed everywhere: respect for the individual, teamwork, and integrity.

The case revealed that the company consistently treated young employees called "analysts" with disrespect and mistrust, which did long-term damage to the firm. Analysts at the firm were top undergraduates from the best universities who were hired to work for the firm for a few years before returning to school to earn their MBA degrees. Because of the abuse, mistrust, and dull work that analysts were forced to endure, the firm had a dreadful record of recruiting them to come back to the firm after they had finished their MBAs, even though senior leaders sought a high "rate of return." Worse yet, former analysts told their fellow MBA students about their bad experiences, making the firm's recruiting efforts more difficult and costly. The students who wrote this case study concluded, "Words seem to have replaced action."

Writing, displaying, and repeating words about treating people with respect, but allowing or encouraging the opposite behavior, is worse than useless. In addition to the well-documented damage inflicted when bullies run amok, an organization and its leaders are seen as hypocrites, which fuels cynicism and scorn. Consider the series of reports in the *St. Petersburg Times* in 2005 about Holland & Knight, a firm with about 1,300 lawyers that had once bragged to the media about its "no jerk rule." The stories reported an internal uproar after managing partner Howell W. Melton Jr. rejected an internal committee's recommendation that partner Douglas A. Wright (from the Tampa office) be given a tough punishment for violating the firm's sexual harassment policy. Melton gave Wright a reprimand instead. A few months later, Melton promoted Wright to the third highest position in the firm.

This promotion happened even though, according to the *Times*, the firm had "made it a priority to weed out selfish, arrogant, and disrespectful attorneys," to enforce what they called a "no jerk rule." And it happened even though nine female attorneys in the Tampa office accused Wright of sexual harassment and the *Daily Business Review* reported that "Wright received a private reprimand last summer, including orders to stop asking women in the office to feel his 'pipes,' or biceps. He also was told to stop commenting on their clothes and sex lives and to forgo any retaliation against the women who'd complained."

According to the *Times*, after managing partner Melton promoted Wright to a leadership role, a leaked seven-page internal e-mail written by Chicago partner Charles D. Knight complained that Holland & Knight had "failed to weed out all of the jerks" and lamented, "Regrettably, it appears that some of them succeeded to the highest levels of the firm's management." Of course, since we weren't inside this firm and have only press reports, it is wise to take these "facts" with a grain of salt. This leak does not, however, appear to be an isolated incident, as another Holland & Knight partner, Mark Stang, wrote an open letter to the *Times* in which he apologized to the "brave women of our firm's Tampa office" and expressed "disgust" with their treatment.

Holland & Knight initially attacked the leak, saying

that it "recklessly and unfairly impugns the reputation of one of the firm's finest partners." Wright also said in a press interview, "I unequivocally deny that I've engaged in sexual harassment with any person here." Wright also asserted that he asked both men and women to feel his "pipes," that "I treat them all the same." Nonetheless, Wright resigned from his management position after the negative stories appeared in the *St. Petersburg Times*, although he remained a partner in the firm. Regardless of exactly what happened inside Holland & Knight, public statements that the firm would weed out disrespectful attorneys backfired from a PR standpoint and outraged at least some partners when the "no jerk rule" was seen as hollow rhetoric.

In contrast, Southwest Airlines has gained both positive press and employee loyalty by demonstrating persistent intolerance for abusive people and even for people who are too cold and gruff to fit with the culture. Southwest tries to screen out people who are cold and unfriendly to fellow employees and to passengers rather than just openly hostile. Ann Rhodes told me about a manager whom Southwest hired who wasn't downright nasty, but was cold and impatient with people. He confided to Ann, "I don't know if I can stand working here. I just want to work with these people; I don't want them as friends." Although Ann worked hard to recruit him because of his skills, she realized he didn't fit at Southwest, so she suggested that he might be happier elsewhere—and he left for a job at another airline a few months later.

Weave the Rule into Hiring and Firing Policies

The lesson from Southwest and JetBlue Airlines is that the no asshole rule needs to be woven into hiring and firing policies. Seattle law firm Perkins Coie, for example, espouses and acts on a "no jerks allowed" rule, which helped earn them a spot on *Fortune*'s "100 Best Companies to Work For" list in 2006 for the fourth year in a row. Consider how the company applies the rule during job interviews. Perkins Coie partners Bob Giles and Mike Reynvaan were once tempted to hire a rainmaker from another firm but realized that doing so would violate the rule. As they put it, "We looked at each other and said, 'What a jerk.' Only we didn't use that word." Reynvaan confirmed that the word they actually used was *asshole*, as is usually the case.

IDEO, one of the most successful innovation firms in the world, also aggressively screens out demeaning and arrogant people. Many candidates are given job offers only after working as interns—people who have demonstrated under real working conditions that they aren't assholes. And when candidates haven't worked with IDEO before, people in the company take the time to filter out assholes. Insider Diego Rodriguez explains:

1. We really value references from people we trust. We also encourage staff to teach university classes and to learn how job candidates perform in the classroom—especially in teams that are under pres-

sure to do good work and do it fast. Not that there's anything wrong with a résumé delivered over the transom, but real references are golden!

2. We try to select for professional competence before people walk in the door so that the interviewing process can focus more on a person's human qualities (or lack thereof).

3. Once in the door, you'll probably speak to a good number of people—more than would seem "reasonable" by most corporate standards. You eat with them. You walk around our offices. You talk. You answer questions. You ask questions. You participate in design exercises. It's all about creating a mutual feeling of "fit."

4. Every candidate is interviewed by people who will be above, below, and alongside them, status-wise. And people from unrelated professional disciplines participate. That way, if you do get hired, you feel that the entire company wants you, not just one specific high-status manager—who, by the way, might or might not be a total asshole. This method also keeps assholes in a hiring position from replicating. Assholes tend to stick together, and once stuck are not easily separated.

Diego's last point is crucial. Research on job interviews and hiring decisions shows that a recruiter tends to hire candidates who look and act like his or her favorite person on the planet—him or herself. Harvard Business School professor Rosabeth Moss Kanter calls this "homosocial re-production," which means that the hiring process (unwit-tingly) causes most organizations to "bring in the clones." *The implication is that assholes will breed like rabbits.* Managers will reproduce themselves in the hiring process, and soon, as Diego says, your organization will have groups domi-nated by assholes—which then start battling other groups or, worse yet, gain power and spread their poison every-where. IDEO battles this tendency by having hiring deci-sions made by a broader group, which works because they have a minuscule percentage of assholes.

For most companies, it is hard enough to resist the temptations to hire bullies who *seem* like they will gener-ate big bucks. It is even more difficult for managers to bring themselves to expel destructive jerks who are al-ready raking in piles of cash. The Men's Wearhouse demonstrates how to back up talk with tangible action. CEO George Zimmer and other executives do more than *talk* about the importance of treating fellow employees with mutual respect, creating a team-selling environ-ment, pleasing every customer, and contributing to the overall success of the store. Men's Wearhouse goes be-yond posting on their Web site statements such as, "Out-standing individual performers rely on teammates to support them in serving the customer. That's why we look at team chemistry when we make hiring, transfer, and promotion decisions."

Consider one example of how George Zimmer demon-strated that this wasn't just lip service. One of the company's more successful salespeople (in terms of dollars in total sales) was eventually fired when, after numerous conversations with him and warnings from management, he still refused to define his own performance partly by the performance of his peers and his store. As Jeff Pfeffer and I learned when writing *The Knowing-Doing Gap*, this salesperson "stole" customers from fellow salespeople, bad-mouthed the firm culture, and was openly opposed to the idea of helping fellow employees with "their" customers. The decision to remove this employee proved that Men's Wearhouse took seriously its values about how people ought to treat one another. It also turned out that firing this selfish and difficult "superstar" had financial benefits, as the total sales volume in the store increased nearly 30% after he left. No single salesperson sold as much as the departed "star," but the store as a whole did better. Apparently, dysfunctional competition and the unpleasant customer experiences generated by this jerk brought out the worst in everyone else.

I've also uncovered cases where, as part of overhauling a broken culture, senior management has purged the organization of these creeps. A senior executive at a Fortune 500 company told me how, in the early 1990s, a new CEO came to his company and promptly launched a campaign to banish twenty-five or so nasty executives. This CEO was determined to get rid of these "known assholes" because they created a "culture of fear" that made the company a place that "was no fun to work at and was unfriendly to customers." The senior executive told me, "It was like he made up 'asshole wanted posters' and put the pictures of these twenty-five guys on them." And "although he wanted to line them up and fire them all at once," the CEO used the performance evaluation system to methodically weed out the people on "the hit list" over a two-year stretch. This purge was a cornerstone of a cultural change that "breathed humanity into the business, for both employees and customers," and helped them break "a lot of other bad habits too, like being afraid to experiment with new ideas." And although I can't reveal the name of this company, I can tell you that during the past decade, it has gone from the middle of the pack to one of the best performers in its industry.

Whether it is just one person or part of a purge, after an incorrigible bully has finally left the building for good, the relief is palpable. When I asked Ann Rhoades about her experience with "easing out" these creeps, she emphasized that in every place she had worked—including airlines, banks, and hotels—a series of predictable events followed. For starters, although these decisions are nearly always difficult to make and often hotly debated, the improvement is so pronounced and rapid that "everyone says, 'why did we wait so long? We should have done it sooner.'" Ann added that people who were on the verge of leaving the company end up staying, and recruiting newcomers to join the group becomes easier. And as the Men's Wearhouse example shows, Ann emphasized that jerks who are supposed to be so valuable that "you couldn't afford to lose them" turn out not to be so valuable and others fill in just fine.

Ann added an interesting twist: the person who takes the jerk's old position is in an enviable position, because "if you are nice at all," people will just be so happy to see you instead of that old wicked tyrant!

Apply the Rule to Customers and Clients

Organizations that are serious about enforcing the no asshole rule apply it to customers, clients, students, and everyone else encountered on the job, not just to employees. They apply the rule to everyone because their people don't deserve the abuse, customers (or taxpayers) aren't paying good money to endure or witness demeaning jerks, and if persistent nastiness from any group is left unchecked, it creates a culture of contempt that infects everyone it touches. The late Joe Gold, the founder of Gold's Gym, which now has more than 550 locations in 43 countries, applied a variation of this rule to customers. He didn't mince words: "To keep it simple, you run your gym like you run your house. Keep it clean and in good running order. No jerks allowed. Members pay on time, and if they give you any crap, throw them out." Gold applied this rule to customers from the time he opened his first gym a block from "Muscle Beach" in Venice Beach, California, where early customers included Arnold Schwarzenegger, who won seven Mr. Olympia titles.

JetBlue and Southwest Airlines put it less colorfully than Gold but apply a similar rule to passengers. Former VP of HR at Southwest, Libby Sartain, explained, "Customer relations sent letters to customers who were abusive to our employees or who lied in their complaints and, on a few occasions, asked them them not to fly on Southwest in the future." The leaders of these companies also back their talk with visible action. One day when Ann Rhoades and another Southwest executive were on a business trip and witnessed a passenger who was berating employees at the check-in counter—swearing at them, hollering, and leaning forward in an intimidating way. Ann's colleague walked up to the counter and told this jerk that everyone would be happier if he flew another airline and that Southwest people don't deserve that kind of treatment, then walked the "irate jerk" over to another airline and bought him a ticket.

Research on how police officers deal with criminals and citizens adds an interesting twist to the rule. MIT professor John Van Maanen spent more than a year doing an intensive anthropological study of police officers in a large city. He attended the police academy and spent months riding with officers to learn about their work. Van Maanen reports in "The Asshole" (a rare scholarly article that uses the 7-letter word) that cops quickly realize that they can't stop every criminal, so they focus on stopping the most demeaning, violent, and immoral of criminals. A veteran cop told Van Maanen, "I guess what our job really boils down to is to not letting the assholes take over the city. What I'm talking about are those shitheads out to prove that they can push everybody around. Those are the assholes we gotta deal with and take care of on patrol. They're the ones that make it tough on decent people out there. You take the majority of what we do and it is nothing more than asshole control."

Van Maanen also found that when citizens became irate or insulting, police officers believed that they deserved the "asshole" label—so the cops dished out punishment ranging from traffic tickets to gruff treatment and even (although unlawful) a bit of roughing up. A "sea story" that cops told illustrates how a citizen might earn the label:

POLICEMAN TO MOTORIST STOPPED FOR SPEEDING: "May I see your driver's license, please?"

MOTORIST: "Why the hell are you picking on me and not somewhere else looking for some real criminals?"

POLICEMAN: "'Cause you are an asshole; that's why. But I didn't know that until you opened your mouth."

Gold's Gym, Southwest and JetBlue Airlines, and police departments all deal with drastically different clientele, but the rule is useful in all three settings because it helps employees stifle a culture of contempt and abuse or, for police, may at least help them stop the worst of it from developing on the streets.

Status and Power Differences: Roots of Many Evils

Leaders in most organizations not only get paid more than others, they also enjoy constant deference and false flattery. A huge body of research—hundreds of studies—

shows that when people are put in positions of power, they start talking more, taking what they want for themselves, ignoring what other people say or want, ignoring how less powerful people react to their behavior, acting more rudely, and generally treating any situation or person as a means for satisfying their own needs—and that being put in positions of power blinds them to the fact that they are acting like jerks.

My Stanford colleague Deborah Gruenfeld has spent years studying and cataloging the effects of putting people in positions where they can lord power over underlings. The idea that power corrupts people and makes them act as if they are above rules meant "for the little people" is widely accepted. But Gruenfeld shows that it is astounding how rapidly even tiny and trivial power advantages can change how people think and act—and usually for the worse. In one experiment, student groups of three discussed a long list of contentious social issues (things like abortion and pollution). One member was (randomly assigned) to the higher power position of evaluating the recommendations made by the other two members. After thirty minutes, the experimenter brought in a plate of five cookies. The more "powerful" students were more likely to take a second cookie, chew with their mouths open, and get crumbs on their faces and the table.

This silly study scares me because it shows how having just a slight power edge causes regular people to grab the goodies for themselves and act like rude pigs. Just think about the effects of holding a position where, in thousands of interactions every year, you are given more than the lion's share of the goodies (not only more pay, but the best suites in the best hotels, meals at the finest restaurants, first-class travel while your underlings fly coach, and on and on), and few people question whether you deserve all those goodies. And if they do complain, you are "protected" by lieutenants who are quick to tell you that those ungrateful whiners don't know what they are talking about.

I was on the receiving end of such boorish behavior a few years ago. It was at a lunch with the CEO of a profitable company who had just been ranked as one of the top corporate leaders by a famous business magazine. He treated our little of group of four or five professors (all fifty-plus-year-old professionals) as if we were naive and rather stupid children. Although, in theory, he was our guest, he told us where to sit and when we could talk (he interrupted several of us in mid-sentence to tell us he had heard enough or didn't care about what we were saying), criticized the food we ordered ("That will make you fat"), and generally conveyed that he was our master and commander and that our job was to focus our efforts on satisfying his every whim.

The most striking part was, just as research on power shows, that he seemed completely oblivious to the fact that he was bullying us and that we were offended. He was astonishingly explicit that his goal was to squeeze as much value out of us as possible; he also kept crediting himself with a host of accomplishments without giving others credit. These actions are consistent with findings that powerful people construe others as a means to one's own ends while simultaneously giving themselves excessive credit for good things that happen to themselves and their organizations. All of us felt oppressed and annoyed by this ogre, but none of us complained to him, let alone confronted him directly. One member of our group nearly lost his temper several times, but had the "sense" to withdraw from the gathering on several occasions and ultimately left early.

Many of the dynamics we experienced at this lunch are reminiscent of what happens in troops of wild baboons. Biologists Robert Sapolsky and Lisa Share have followed a troop of wild baboons in Kenya since 1978. Sapolsky and Share called them "the Garbage Dump Troop" because they got much of their food from a garbage pit at a tourist lodge. But not every baboon was allowed to eat from the pit in the early 1980s: the aggressive, high-status males in the troop refused to allow lower-status males or any females to eat the garbage. Between 1983 and 1986, infected meat from the dump led to the deaths of 46% of the adult males in the troop. The biggest and meanest males died. As in other baboon troops studied, before they died, these top-ranking males routinely bit, bullied, and chased males of similar and lower status, and occasionally directed their aggression at females.

But when the top ranking males died, aggression by the new top baboons dropped dramatically, with most aggression occurring between baboons of similar rank, little of it directed toward lower-status males, and none at all directed at females. Troop members also spent a larger percentage of the time grooming and sat closer together than in the past, and hormone samples indicated that the lowest-status males experienced less stress than underlings in other baboon troops. Most interestingly, these effects persisted at least through the late 1990s, well after all the original "kinder" males had died. Not only that, when adolescent males who grew up in other troops joined the Garbage Dump Troop, they too engaged in less aggressive behavior than in other baboon troops. As Sapolsky put it, "We don't understand the mechanism of transmission . . . but the jerky new guys are obviously learning: we don't do things like that around here." So, at least by baboon standards, the Garbage Dump Troop developed and enforced what I would call a no asshole rule.

I am not suggesting that you get rid of all the alpha males in your organization, as tempting as that may be at times. The lesson from the baboons is that when the social distance between higher- and lower-status mammals in a group is reduced and steps are taken to keep the distance smaller, higher-status members are less likely to act like jerks. Human leaders can use this lesson to avoid turning into mean, selfish, and insensitive jerks, too. Despite all the trappings, some leaders do remain attuned to how people around them are *really* feeling, to what their employees *really* believe about how the organization is run, and to what customers *really* think about their company's products and services. As the Garbage Dump Troop teaches us, the key thing these leaders do is take potent and constant steps that dampen rather than amplify the power differences between themselves and others (both inside and outside the company).

Pay is a vivid sign of power differences, and a host of studies suggest that when the difference between the highest- and lowest-paid people in a company or team is reduced, a host of good things happen—including improved financial performance, better product quality, enhanced research productivity, and, in baseball teams, a better win-loss record. But the idea of reducing pay differences isn't catching on. Despite such findings, the CEO of a typical large corporation makes more than five hundred times what the average worker earns. Yet reducing this distance sends the message to both the CEO and the average worker that they are not superstars or superior beings.

Consider James D. Sinegal, co-founder and CEO of Costco, a warehouse retailer. His salary in 2003 was $350,000, which is just about ten times what is earned by his top hourly employees and roughly double that of a typical Costco store manager. Costco also pays 92.5% of employee health-care costs. Sinegal could take a lot more goodies for himself, but has refused a bonus in profitable years because "we didn't meet the standards that we had set for ourselves," and he has sold only a modest percentage of his stock over the years. Even Costco's compensation committee acknowledges that he is underpaid.

Sinegal believes that by taking care of his people and

staying close to them, they will provide better customer service, Costco will be more profitable, and everyone (including shareholders like himself) will win. Sinegal takes other steps to reduce the "power distance" between himself and other employees. He visits hundreds of Costco stores a year, constantly mixing with the employees as they work and asking questions about how he can make things better for them and Costco customers. Despite continuing skepticism from analysts about wasting money on labor costs, Costco's earnings, profits, and stock price continue to rise. Treating employees fairly also helps the bottom line in other ways, as Costco's "shrinkage rate" (theft by employees and customers) is only two-tenths of 1%; other retail chains suffer ten to fifteen times the amount. Sinegal just sees all this as good business because, when you are a CEO, "everybody is watching you every minute anyway. If they think the message you're sending is phony, they are going to say, 'Who does he think he is?' "

Sinegal is the rare CEO who can bring himself to reduce the social distance between himself and everyone else in the company. In the United States and other Western countries, we are always pressing to create bigger differences among winners, also-rans, and losers, but if you want to have fewer assholes—and better organizational performance—reducing the differences between the highest- and lowest-status members of your organization is the way to go. This doesn't mean that organizations should strive to eliminate all status differences between members;

on the contrary, some people are more important to the organization than others because they are more difficult to replace or have more essential skills. Status differences will always be with us, and even at a place like Costco, CEO Sinegal is still at the top of the heap, and the guy who sweeps the parking lot is near the bottom. George Zimmer is the top dog at Men's Wearhouse, and a rookie "sales consultant" is near the bottom. But look at what these and other leaders do to build organizations with fewer assholes and spark better performance—they embrace what I call the *power-performance paradox*: they realize that their company has and should have a pecking order, but they do everything they can to downplay and reduce status and power differences among members.

Focus on Conversations and Interactions

In chapter 1, I described a workplace aggression survey in the U.S. Department of Veterans Affairs. It was part of a big organizational change—involving more than seven thousand people at eleven VA sites—aimed at reducing employee bullying, psychological abuse, and aggression. Each site had an "action team" of managers and union members that developed a custom intervention. But there were key similarities at each site: people learned about the damage that aggression does, used role-playing exercises to "get in the shoes" of bullies and victims, and reflected before and after they acted. Action team members and local VA leaders also made a public commitment to model civilized behavior. The teams focused on making small but good changes at each place. At one site, managers and employees worked to eliminate seemingly small slights like glaring, interruptions, and treating people as if they were "invisible"—slights that had escalated into big problems in the past. At another, they held something they called a "flake-off" every Friday afternoon, where the group drilled into the little details of big problems—such as having veterans talk about "what it is like to be me" and "how you could help me more."

The "business results" included less overtime and sick leave, fewer employee complaints, and shorter patient waiting times. There were also signs of increased productivity at several sites. Productivity went up 9% at the Houston Cemetery—as measured by the number of burials per worker. It also turned out that focusing on the little things that people did was, as I would put it, a remarkably effective asshole management technique. Surveys done before (November 2000) and after (November 2002) revealed that these interventions found substantial drops in thirty-two of sixty kinds of bullying across the eleven sites—things like glaring, swearing, "the silent treatment," obscene gestures, yelling and shouting, physical threats and assaults, temper tantrums, vicious rumors and gossip, threats of physical harm, and sexist and racist remarks. At the Houston Cemetery, for example, employees reported a 31% decrease in "total reported acts of aggression." Project manager James Scaringi told me that as of 2006, most of these programs still persist and that spin-off interventions were cropping up throughout the VA (which has about 220,000 employees), including one focused on workplace civility and another that teaches people how to stop small conflicts from exploding into big problems.

The lesson from what I believe is the biggest bullying intervention ever done in the United States is that small, seemingly trivial changes in how people think, talk, and act can add up to some mighty big effects in the end. As Scaringi told me, "Some of us were skeptical at first that such little changes could make a difference, but the evidence convinced us otherwise."

Teach People How to Fight

As noted earlier, enforcing a no asshole rule doesn't mean turning your organization into a paradise for conflict-averse wimps. The best groups and organizations—especially the most creative ones—are places where people know how to fight. At Intel, the largest semiconductor maker in the world, all full-time employees are given training in "constructive confrontation," a hallmark of the company culture. Leaders and corporate trainers emphasize that bad things happen when "the bullies win," when fighting means personal attacks, disrespect, and rude intimidation. These ill effects include "only the loudest and strongest voices get heard," "no diversity of views," poor communication, high tension, low productivity, and the belief that people are first "resigned" to living with the nastiness and then "resign" from the company. Intel preaches that *the only thing worse than too much confrontation is no confrontation at all.* So the company teaches employees how to approach people and problems positively, to use evidence and logic, and to attack problems and not people.

The University of Michigan's Karl Weick advises, "Fight as if you are right; listen as if you are wrong." That is what Intel tries to teach through initial lectures, role playing, and, most essential, the ways in which managers and leaders fight. They teach people *how* to fight and *when* to fight. Their motto is "Disagree and then commit," because second-guessing, complaining, and arguing after a decision is made saps effort and attention—which obscures whether a decision is failing because it is a bad idea or it is a good idea that is implemented with insufficient energy and commitment. People are also taught to delay their arguments until all the key facts are in, because it wastes time and because taking a public stance based on incomplete information leads people to defend and publicly commit to paths that ultimately clash with the best evidence.

Intel's approach is backed by a series of experiments and field studies done at the Kellogg Business School, Wharton Business School, and Stanford showing that destructive conflict is typically "emotional," "interpersonal," or "relationship-based" when people fight because they despise one another and, in some cases, have a history of trying to harm one another. Groups that fight in these ways are less effective at both creative and routine tasks, and their people are constantly upset and demoralized. In contrast, these researchers find that conflict is constructive when people argue over ideas rather than personality or relationship issues, which they call "task" or "intellectual" conflict. Stanford's Kathleen Eisenhardt and her colleagues, for example, found that constructive conflict results when top management teams "base discussion on current factual information" and "develop multiple alternatives to enrich the debate." Healthy arguments like these were hallmarks of a team led by Bob Taylor at Xerox PARC in the 1970s that was credited with developing many technologies that made the computer revolution possible (including the personal computer and laser printing). Michael Hiltzik's book on these magical years at PARC, *Dealers of Lightning*, describes Taylor's leadership style: "Impugning a man's thinking was acceptable, but never his character. Taylor strived to create a democracy where everyone's ideas were impartially subject to the group's learned demolition, regardless of the proponent's credentials or rank."

Beware, however, that all these pretty stories and sanitized research findings mask how messy and difficult it can be to fight with other people over ideas without acting like an asshole. I struggle with this challenge constantly. Jeff Pfeffer is my most frequent coauthor (we've written two books and many articles) and one of my most trusted friends. We both say, and believe, that "the more we fight, the better we write." Yet when Jeff criticizes one of my ideas (which happens several hundred times a year), my first reaction is often "that asshole," and I have to take a moment, calm down, and then respond to his logic and facts.

At the moment, I am feeling similar tensions in a start-up team that I am part of at the Hasso Plattner Institute of Design at Stanford, a diverse group of experienced designers, managers, executives, students, and traditional faculty like me who are trying to spread design thinking and develop more collaborative and creative ways of teaching classes. We even have a therapist—we call him the "d.shrink"—who goes to our meetings and helps us resolve tensions and move forward. Despite our shared goals, mutual respect, and help from the d.shrink, I've had multiple incidents where I thought that I was involved in "constructive" confrontation but later found out that I had hurt someone's feelings. And I recently had the experience where a fellow faculty member made a great suggestion to improve my class. Rather than listening as if I was wrong, I responded by writing a nasty e-mail that contained several snide personal comments. Fortunately, I decided not to send it, went off and calmed down (and had a nice glass of wine), thought about it, and realized he was right. I followed his suggestion (essentially that we give the students more time and personal attention during their project presentations), and the class was a big success. Other times, I find myself holding back on making critical comments that I believe will help the group but that I fear will generate too much anger. My point is that as we travel from moment to moment, and group to group, finding the sweet spot between being constructive enough and critical enough is tough, and as life is confusing and messy, we all will make mistakes along the way.

A few years back, I ran a management workshop with a group of about twenty-five senior Intel executives. I asked them what it was like to engage in effective constructive confrontation. They answered that on the whole, it makes them a far more effective company, but it was a constant struggle to make it work, as some teams would "swerve" toward destructive confrontation, with personal attacks and other nastiness becoming pervasive during meetings, while other teams would "swerve" in the opposite direction, turning into timid and conflict-adverse wimps. The advice from the Intel executives was similar to the lessons learned during the organizational change effort at VA sites. Having a policy and some training isn't enough; to have effective interactions, you've got to focus on what is happening in every conversation and meeting you have, tweak what you and others do "in the moment," and constantly reflect about the little things that happen.

Should It Be "the One Asshole Rule"?

Decades of research on how human groups react to "deviant" members implies that having one or two assholes around may be better than having none at all. A series of clever studies on littering by the University of Arizona's Robert Cialdini shows how having one conspicuous rule-breaker can spur others to do the right thing. In one study, Cialdini's research assistants created a "condition" where they spewed "an assortment of handbills, candy wrappers, cigarette butts, and paper cups" around a small enclosed parking lot. In the other "condition," they cleaned the lot carefully so that there was no litter at all. They placed a large handbill under the windshield wiper on the driver's side of each car that said, "THIS IS AUTOMOTIVE SAFETY WEEK. PLEASE DRIVE CAREFULLY," which the driver had to remove to see out the front window.

The question was what did the driver do with the handbill? Did he or she walk over to the garbage can or throw it on the ground? It turned out that drivers were more likely to litter when the setting was already a mess. But here is the twist: half of the drivers encountered a researcher acting as a "confederate" (just as they got off the elevator) who conspicuously first read the handbill and then threw it on the ground. The effect of watching this one "jerk" violate the littering norm was intriguing— drivers who saw the "norm violation" were less likely to throw their handbill into a clean parking lot (6% vs. 14%) but more likely to throw it into a messy lot (54% vs. 32%).

The lesson is that when we see someone break a known rule—like "Don't litter"—and no one else seems to be breaking it, that single "deviant act" sticks out, which makes the rule more vivid and powerful in our minds. But when we see a person break a rule and everyone else seems to be breaking it, we are even more likely to break the rule, too—because there is evidence that we can get away with it, or even are expected to break the espoused rule. Cialdini's other studies showed that although people are generally less likely to litter when a place is clean rather than messy, *they are less likely to litter when there is one piece of garbage on the ground rather than no garbage at all.* Again, the same principle shows that when one person or perhaps two people break a known rule, we are actually more likely to carefully follow it than when no one breaks it—because the stark contrast between the bad behavior of a single "deviant" makes everyone else's "good behavior" more vivid in our minds.

Cialdini's findings are consistent with research on deviants and social norms, which shows that when one or two "bad apples" are kept around—and perhaps rejected, punished, and shunned—everyone else is more conscientious about following the written or unwritten rules. The implication for building a civilized workplace is that if one or two jerks and bullies are working there and not rewarded for their actions, other organization members will be more diligent about adhering to the no asshole rule. A "token asshole" reminds everyone how not to behave and the unpleasant consequences for breaking the rule.

I don't know of any organizations that hire token jerks on purpose, but I've worked in and with a few organizations that have accidentally hired one or two who then have gone on to (unwittingly) demonstrate to everyone else how *not* to behave. No matter how carefully organizations screen candidates, some people turn nasty for personal reasons (that may have nothing to do with the job), and some can hide their dark side until after they are hired or even until they are promoted to tenured professor, partner, or perhaps your boss. As I wrote in my *Harvard Business Review* essay, "So by aiming to hire no assholes at all, you just might get the one or two that you need." One e-mail that I got in response, from a consultant in a large professional services firm, added a wise twist: "I agree that you need one jerk around, but everyone should know where the jerk fits. [The jerk] sure as hell shouldn't be promoted." This consultant is on target. After all, if you keep one or two of these token assholes around, then you want to make crystal clear that their behavior is *wrong*.

Warning: Be Slow to Brand People

A few years back, I was talking to Peter Macdonald, one of IDEO's veteran engineers. He was talking about several of the gruffer people at IDEO, people who are known in some corners as being jerks. Peter then went on to say that IDEO was actually quite effective at keeping jerks out of the company, but newcomers sometimes mistake people who are gruff, are outspoken, and insist on applying high standards to their own work and everyone else's as being demeaning, nasty people. Peter went on to say, "Whenever I've worked with a person who was supposed to be an asshole, I always found out that it was a bad rap; each turned out to be okay once I got to know [him or her] better."

Peter's experience at IDEO implies multiple lessons for effective asshole management. First, resist the temptation to apply the label to anyone who annoys you or has a bad moment. If you apply the label to everyone, it means nothing. Second, be slow to brand people as certified assholes just because they act like temporary assholes now and then or have a gruff exterior. Some people with the roughest exteriors have the biggest hearts once you get to know them—I call them porcupines with hearts of gold. When a person rarely smiles, has a hard time looking others in the eye, or seems to have a permanent sneer, our natural reaction is to label him or her as a jerk. As Peter learned, it is best to withhold your judgment and watch what they actually do—to focus on how they treat people on other dimensions, especially how they treat people with less power and status. Third, the best way to overcome a negative stereotype of someone—unfounded beliefs that a person or all people in some category are evil, lazy, stupid, or whatever—is to work on a task with that person that entails mutual and successful cooperation toward some goal. Existing research focuses on using this method to overcome ethnic and racial stereotypes, but as Peter's experience shows, this method can extend to overcoming the belief that a particular colleague is a jerk or is part of a group (e.g., lawyers) that is stereotyped as containing "all" assholes. Of course, there are some people who fail all these tests; the more we know about them, the more evidence we get that they are certified assholes. But it is wise to make such judgments on better rather than worse evidence.

The Upshot: Enforce the Rule by Linking Big Policies to Small Decencies

Effective asshole management entails an interplay, fueling a virtuous, self-reinforcing cycle between the "big" things that organizations do—the stated philosophies; the written policies; the training and official hiring, firing, and reward practices—and the smaller ways in which people actually treat one another.

We saw the big policies at Southwest, like hiring and firing people for their attitudes and banning incorrigible passengers, which were reflected in and reinforced by the smaller things that leaders did. Recall how Herb Kelleher refused to hire the pilot who was nasty to a receptionist, how Ann Rhoades encouraged an unfriendly manager to find another job, and how another executive bought a nasty passenger a ticket on another airline. I've distilled my main ideas into the attached list of top ten steps that organizations and their leaders can take to enforce the rule. To boil it down even further: Having all the right business philosophies and management practices to support the no asshole rule is meaningless unless you treat the person *right in front of you, right now, in the right way.*

THE TOP TEN STEPS

Enforcing the No Asshole Rule

1. **Say the rule, write it down, and act on it.** But if you can't or won't follow the rule, it is better to say nothing at all—avoiding a false claim is the lesser of two evils. You don't want to be known as a hypocrite *and* the leader of an organization that is filled with assholes.

2. **Assholes will hire other assholes.** Keep your resident jerks out of the hiring process, or if you can't, involve as many "civilized" people in interviews and decisions to offset this predilection of people to hire "jerks like me."

3. **Get rid of assholes fast.** Organizations usually wait too long to get rid of certified and incorrigible assholes, and once they do, the reaction is usually, "Why did we wait so long to do that?"

4. **Treat certified assholes as incompetent employees.** Even if people do other things extraordinary well but persistently demean others, they ought to be treated as incompetent.

5. **Power breeds nastiness.** Beware that giving people—even seemingly nice and sensitive people— even a little power can turn them into big jerks.

6. **Embrace the power-performance paradox.** Accept that your organization does have and should have a pecking order, but do everything you can to downplay and reduce unnecessary status differences among members. The result will be fewer assholes and, according to the best studies, better performance, too.

7. **Manage moments—not just practices, policies, and systems.** Effective asshole management means focusing on and changing the little things that you and your people do—and big changes will follow. Reflect on what you do, watch how others respond to you and to one another, and work on "tweaking" what happens as you are interacting with the person *in front of you right now.*

8. **Model and teach constructive confrontation.** Develop a culture where people know when to argue and when to stop fighting and, instead, gather more evi-

dence, listen to other people, or stop whining and implement a decision (even if they still disagree with it). When the time is ripe to battle over ideas, follow Karl Weick's advice: fight as if you are right; listen as if you are wrong.

9. **Adopt the one asshole rule.** Because people follow rules and norms better when there are rare or occasional examples of bad behavior, no asshole rules might be most closely followed in organizations that permit one or two token jerks to hang around. These "reverse role models" remind everyone else of the *wrong* behavior.

10. **The bottom line: link big policies to small decencies.** Effective asshole management happens when there is a virtuous, self-reinforcing cycle between the "big" things that organizations do and the little things that happen when people talk to one another and work together.

I also want to emphasize that the true test of an organization's no asshole rule comes when things are going badly. It is easy to be civilized when things are going well, when you've experienced one success after another and the money and praise are rolling in. As noted, during the years of Google's wild growth, the company has been guided by the motto "Don't be evil." Recall that senior vice president Shona Brown explained that the motto meant, in part, that it wasn't efficient to be an asshole at Google. Unnecessary nastiness has been a big no-no at Google from the earliest days when Larry Page and

Sergey Brin started the company. I hope this norm persists as the company continues to mature and hits (inevitable) financial rough spots. Unfortunately, some companies turn nasty when things get rough. But it doesn't need to be that way.

Xilinx, a semiconductor firm led by CEO Wim Roelandts, continued to be a civilized workplace after revenues plummeted more than 50% in 2001, in part because Roelandts treated every employee with so much respect—talking to people at all levels, inviting them into his office, and quickly answering each worried e-mail with factual information. As one employee said, "I am encouraged to take my questions about anything directly to the CEO. Every time I have, he returns my messages within a day." Xilinx's humane treatment of people— which included avoiding layoffs through pay cuts and voluntary termination programs—led people to bond together rather than turn mean during the crisis. The company bounced back financially by 2003; even more impressive was that before the trouble started, Xilinx ranked twenty-first on *Fortune*'s "100 Best Companies to Work For" in 2000. Xilinx managed to climb to sixth in 2001 (during the worst of it) and was ranked fourth in 2002.

Treating people with respect rather than contempt makes good business sense—although it won't always be enough to help save a troubled company. We can never know what the future will bring to our organizations and our lives. But if you work with other people, you know with 100% certainty that your days will be filled with face-to-face and phone conversations, e-mail exchanges, meetings, and other kinds of human interactions—and that your moments, hours, and days at work will be more meaningful, peaceful, and fun if you work in a place where the no asshole rule reigns supreme.

CHAPTER 4

How to Stop Your "Inner Jerk" from Getting Out

The last chapter was about applying the rule to organizations. This one is about applying it to yourself—about keeping your "inner jerk" from rearing its ugly head. Some people act like assholes no matter where they go. They can't keep their disdain and rage from polluting even the most peaceful, warm, and loving places. If you are all asshole all the time, you probably need therapy, Prozac, anger management classes, transcendental mediation, more exercise, or all of the above. The combined contributions of coworkers and loved ones, therapists of all stripes, and the pharmaceutical industry help many of us keep our nastiness in check. Yet most of us, even the most "naturally" kind and mentally healthy, can turn caustic and cruel under the wrong conditions. Human emotions, including anger, contempt, and fear, are remarkably contagious. The

prevalence of bullies in most organizations, plus the pressures of most jobs, makes it difficult to get through the
workday without (at least occasionally) igniting or becoming trapped in episodes that turn us into menacing creeps.

Yet there are ways to quell your contempt. The first
step is to view acting like an asshole as a communicable
disease. Once you unleash disdain, anger, and contempt
or someone unleashes it on you, it spreads like wildfire.
"Emotional contagion" researcher Elaine Hatfield and her
colleagues concluded, "In conversation, people tend auto-
matically and continuously to mimic and synchronize their
movements with the facial expressions, voices, postures,
movements, and instrumental behaviors of others." If you
display contempt, others (even spectators—not just your
targets) will respond in much the same way, igniting a vicious circle that can turn everyone around you into a
mean-spirited monster just like you.

Experiments by Leigh Thompson and Cameron Ander-
son show that even when compassionate people join a
group with a leader who is "high-energy, aggressive,
mean, the classic bully type," they are "temporarily transformed into carbon copies of the alpha dogs." Evidence
that nastiness is an infectious disease that you can catch
from your boss isn't confined to laboratory studies. Dr.
Michelle Duffy followed a sample of 177 hospital workers
to see the effects of "morally disengaged" bosses who
were insensitive to others and who condoned teasing,
put-downs, and coldness toward colleagues. Duffy found
that six months later, people who worked for a nasty boss

often became jerks, too. As Duffy told the *New York Times*, "This moral disengagement spreads like a germ." Contagion studies also show that when people "catch" unpleasant expressions from others, like frowning or glaring, it makes them feel grumpier and angrier—even though they don't realize or deny that it is happening to them. So being around people who *look* angry makes you *feel* angry, too. Hatfield and her colleagues sum up emotional contagion research with an Arabic proverb: "A wise man associating with the vicious becomes an idiot."

A swarm of assholes is like a "civility vacuum," sucking the warmth and kindness out of everyone who enters and replacing it with coldness and contempt. These dangers are reflected in some wise advice that I heard from the late Bill Lazier, a successful executive who spent the last twenty years of his career teaching business and entrepreneurship at Stanford. Bill said that when you get a job offer or join a team, take a close look at the people you would work with, not just at whether they are successful or not. He warned that if your future colleagues are self-centered, nasty, narrow-minded, unethical, or overworked and physically ill, there is little chance that you will turn them into better human beings or transform it into a healthy workplace—even a tiny company. If you join a group filled with jerks, odds are that you will catch their disease.

Unfortunately, I learned this lesson after joining a group led by a renowned management guru. It was during the height of the dot-com boom in Silicon Valley, a time when arrogance, selfishness, and the unstated belief that if you can't get rich now, you must not be very smart rippled throughout the region. Our little group met several Sundays in a row to talk about starting a business strategy Web site. About seven or eight people attended these meetings, but the bad behavior was confined to only four of us—the guru, two other management experts, and me. We each vied to establish our position as the alpha male. We also did nearly all the talking; the women and younger men at the meeting rarely spoke, and when they tried, we ignored or interrupted them and went back to our pathetic game of status jousting.

There was a veneer of civility, but it barely masked our intense and obnoxious one-upmanship. We were al-legedly coming up with ideas for the company (which never got off the ground), and instead, we spent the meet-ings showing off our knowledge, bragging about our ac-complishments, and using interruptions and rapid-fire talk to battle for airtime. One management consultant whom I know describes meetings like these as "like watching apes in the zoo throwing feces to assert dominance."

That pretty much sums up what we did. I felt like an asshole at the end of each meeting, and that feeling was well deserved. My wife, Marina, pointed out that when I came home from each gathering, I acted like an overbear-ing and pompous jerk there, too. As she put it, I was suf-fering from a bad case of "testosterone poisoning." I eventually came to my senses and realized—to put it another way—that I had caught and fueled an epidemic of "asshole poisoning." So I quit the group.

I like to think of myself as such a good, moral, and strong-willed person that I am immune from mimicking the mean-spirited morons around me. You probably do, too. Unfortunately, as mountains of evidence and Bill Lazier's advice suggest, asshole poisoning is a contagious disease that anyone can catch. That's the bad news. The good news is that we are not powerless pawns who—as soon as we find ourselves knee-deep in assholes—are condemned to become caustic and cruel clones.

How to Avoid "Asshole Poisoning"

DON'T JOIN THE JERKS—LEONARDO DA VINCI GOT IT RIGHT

Bill Lazier's advice means that you ought to do your homework before taking a job. Find out if you are about to enter a den of assholes, and if you are, don't give in to the temptation to join them in the first place. Leonardo da Vinci said, "It is easier to resist at the beginning than at the end," which is sound social psychology. The more time and effort that people put into anything—no matter how useless, dysfunctional, or downright stupid it might be— the harder it is for them to walk away, be it a bad investment, a destructive relationship, an exploitive job, or a workplace filled with browbeaters, bullies, and bastards.

Although most people know that sunk costs shouldn't

be considered in making a decision, the "too-much-invested-to-quit syndrome" is a powerful driver of human behavior. We justify all the time, effort, suffering, and years and years that we devote to something by telling ourselves and others that there must be something worth-while and important about it or we never would have sunk so much of our lives into it. And there is a double whammy: the more time that we spend knee-deep in nasty people, the more prone we are to become just like them.

I could have saved myself a lot of aggravation if I'd followed "da Vinci's rule" before joining that group led by the management guru. I knew he was an arrogant and overbearing jerk when I agreed to go to those meetings—I had been to earlier meetings with him on projects where I had caught asshole poisoning. Yet I couldn't help myself; my greed for money and status overwhelmed that little voice inside me that was saying, "You are going to act like a jerk if you do it." I eventually did come to my senses. At least I backed out before investing a lot of time and effort and falling prey to the too-much-invested-to-quit syndrome.

Sometimes da Vinci's rule can save you from a work-place where people have fooled you during job interviews and the recruitment process but start showing their true colors before you take the job. Consider what happened to a friend and colleague of mine. I'll call her Andrea. She was offered what sounded like a fabulous job working with a respected scientist. When the scientist was wooing her to accept the job of leading a groundbreaking new program, he promised Andrea that they would work closely together and that he would give her freedom and professional respect. He raved about her past experience managing similar programs, treated her with warmth, and was downright charming. Yet the scientist showed his true colors right after Andrea accepted her "dream" position, but before her official start date. She was so excited about the new job that she started going to meetings with him and his colleagues. During these meetings, the scientist didn't introduce her to the team, interrupted her repeatedly, and belittled her ideas. Although she was hired to set the strategy, she was told, "Just get on the chairlift while it is moving." When Andrea asked to meet with the scientist to discuss her concerns, he wouldn't take the time. Andrea wisely pulled the plug on the position.

My wife, Marina, had a similar experience about twenty years ago when she was a young lawyer. After she had accepted a job in which she would be working for a renowned litigation attorney, Marina met a young lawyer from that firm who "outed" the renowned attorney as a flaming asshole. When the attorney heard from the firm's recruiters that Marina had changed her mind because he was "difficult to work with," he called Marina to berate and criticize her and to pressure her to reveal the insider who had outed him. Marina refused to reveal her source, and the litigator became even more hostile when she told him, "Your behavior on this call confirms the reasons behind my decision."

It would have been a lot easier on Andrea and Marina if they had done more homework in advance. Yet they were wise to "resist at the beginning," both to spare themselves the abuse and to avoid joining a workplace where they could catch asshole poisoning.

WALK OUT—OR STAY AWAY AS MUCH AS YOU CAN

It isn't always possible to know what a place will be like before you start a job. The people who recruit you might put on fake charm during interviews (like the scientist did to Andrea) or use a bait-and-switch technique where they roll out delightful people to recruit you and then—after you sign on—put you in an obnoxious group. Or the job may be so stressful—with long hours, severe time pressures, or cruel clients—that you can't contain your anxiety and anger. Again, da Vinci's rule works: get out as fast as you can.

An account by waitress Jessica Seaver shows how this can happen in a fascinating book called *Gig*, a collection of more than 120 interviews in which American workers talk about their jobs. Seaver reports that she learned how to deal with customers "when their attitude is just so piss-poor or they're just high on themselves" by avoiding them and—most of the time—containing her rage. But Seaver reached her breaking point at one packed and noisy bar after working six days in a row. A drunk from Alabama ordered round after round of drinks for his friends and never gave her a tip. After he ordered yet another round of tequila shots, Seaver "doused his head with salt" and told the drunk, "You know, if you don't start tipping me pretty soon here, you can just walk your ass up to the bar, 'cause I've sold you at least a hundred fifty bucks of product and you've been stiffing me." Seaver soon left for a "mellow" place where the risk of asshole poisoning was a lot lower.

Seaver's instinct was to avoid this jerk, but she couldn't because he was sitting smack in the middle of her section. Her inclination brings up a related tactic: if you can't or won't quit your job, do everything you can to limit your contact with the worst people. Go to as few meetings with known assholes as possible, answer inquires from them as slowly and rarely as you can, and when you can't avoid them, keep the meetings short. I'll talk about avoidance tactics in chapter 5 too, as they are essential for surviving a corrosive workplace that you can't or won't leave. But hiding and walking away can also limit your risk of catching and spreading bad cheer. To do so, you may need to unlearn what we were all taught in grade school: that the "good kids" stay in their seats and endure everything from mind-numbing boredom to demeaning teachers.

As adults, many of us still can't shake off that lesson. We feel glued to our chairs during conversations and meetings with nasty people. Listen to author Nick Hornby when he gives "one of the only pieces of advice that I have to offer younger generations: *you're allowed to walk out.*" Hornby was talking about boring concerts and movies, but also suggests it is good advice for any occasion—and

to me, that includes when you feel surrounded by a
bunch of assholes.

WARNING: SEEING COWORKERS AS RIVALS AND
ENEMIES IS A DANGEROUS GAME

As we saw in the last chapter, when status differences
between people (and baboons) at the top, middle, and
bottom of the pecking order are emphasized and magnified, it brings out the worst in everyone. Alpha males and
females turn into selfish and insensitive jerks and subject
their underlings to abuse; people at the bottom of the
heap withdraw, suffer psychological damage, and perform
at levels well below their actual abilities. Many organizations amplify these problems by constantly rating and
ranking people, giving the spoils to a few stars, and treating the rest as second- and third-class citizens. The unfortunate result is that people who ought to be friends
become enemies, cutthroat jerks who run wild as they
scramble to push themselves up the ladder and push their
rivals down.

Yet believing that organizational life is pure cutthroat
competition is a dangerous half-truth. It is nearly always a
blend of cooperation and competition, and organizations
that forbid extreme internal competition not only are more
civilized, but perform better too—despite societal myths
to the contrary. And from a personal point of view, if you
look at the odds, when you link your self-worth to becoming top dog and staying at the top of the heap, you are

playing a game that you will probably lose. The odds are against you that you will be the top salesperson, best baseball player, or CEO, and even if you are, you will eventually lose your crown. Winning is a wonderful thing if you can help and respect others along the way. But if you stomp on others as you climb the ladder and treat them like losers once you reach the top, my opinion is that you debase your own humanity and undermine your team or organization.

Research on "framing" by social psychologists suggests a few tricks you can use to avoid being an overly competitive jerk and to help immunize yourself from catching asshole poisoning. The assumptions and language we use—the lenses that we see the world through—can have big effects on how we treat others. Even seemingly small differences in language that we hear and use can determine whether we cooperate or compete. Stanford researcher Lee Ross and his colleagues published experiments in the *Journal of Experimental Psychology* and *Personality and Social Psychology Bulletin* in which they had pairs of students play a game where they could choose to cooperate and treat it as a "win-win" game or compete and treat it as a competitive "I win, you lose" game.

The games were based on the classic prisoner's dilemma. If both parties were honest and cooperative, both were rewarded well and equally. If both were competitive, then both got screwed with a low score. If one person competed but the other cooperated, then the competing person won big with a big score and the cooperative person got screwed with a very low score. People who don't cooperate in prisoner's-dilemma situations often lie, telling their partner that they are going to cooperate but then turning against their partner in the end to grab all of the goodies for themselves. Prisoner's-dilemma situations have been used in thousands of experiments and mathematical simulations, including work done by several Nobel Prize winners.

In Ross's experiments, the only difference between the two games was that half of the players were told that it was the "Community Game" (conjuring up images of shared fate and collaboration) and the other half were told that it was the "Wall Street Game" (conjuring up images of a dog-eat-dog world). People who played the Community Game were dramatically more cooperative and honest about their intentions than those who believed they were playing the Wall Street Game. These findings were later replicated with U.S. Air Force Academy cadets, and related experiments show that when people are first exposed to or "primed" with words like *enemy*, *battle*, *inconsiderate*, *vicious*, *lawyer*, and *capitalist*, they were far less likely to cooperate than when first exposed to words like *helped*, *fair*, *warm*, *mutual*, and *share*. So these seemingly trivial differences in language had profound effects on how willing people were to be selfish and dishonest backstabbers.

The implications of framing life as a purely competitive game can be seen in the advice that James Halpin, former CEO of CompUSA, gave his people: "Your coworkers are your competition" and "I tell employees to ask themselves at the end of each day, 'What did I do to put myself above my coworkers?' If you can't come up with anything, you wasted a day." Halpin told the *Academy of Management Executive* that he turned this philosophy into action at meetings with the twenty regional managers of this chain of retail stores. Halpin said that he drew a line down the center of the table: the ten strongest performers sat behind the line; the ten weakest performers sat in front of the line, closer to where senior managers stood, "because they have to listen to everything we've got to say." These managers also wore name tags that displayed the shrink numbers (lost and stolen inventory) for the stores they ran. Halpin believed that the proper reaction to poor numbers should be, "Look at the guy's shrink. It is terrible compared to the company average. I am not sitting next to him." Halpin never mentioned the alternative frame: when people who do things well give help and advice to people who do it badly, the whole organization can benefit. Halpin was eventually forced out after CompUSA suffered financial problems, but I've always been intrigued by this case because it shows how the way in which the world is framed can shape how people behave. Halpin was—quite intentionally—creating a world where cutthroat competition was expected and seen as desirable. The implication is that if you want to quell your inner jerk and avoid spreading (and catching) this form of asshole poisoning, use ideas and language that frame life in ways that will make you focus on cooperation. Consider three "cooperative frames" that you might use.

First, although many situations do require a mix of competition and cooperation, try focusing on the win-win aspects. When I visit organizations, in order to get a sense of how cooperative or competitive people are, I listen carefully to the words they use. I listen for the word *we* versus *I* and *me*. I also pay close attention to how the people talk about their view of other groups in the organization—do they still say *we*, or do they start saying *us* versus *them*? These sound like trivial things, but as Alan Kay and Lee Ross showed, small differences in language can be diagnostic.

Renowned management guru Peter F. Drucker looked back at his 65-year consulting career shortly before he died. He concluded that great leaders could be either "charismatic or dull" or "visionary or numbers-oriented," but the most inspiring and effective managers he knew all had a few things in common, including, "They thought and said *we* rather than *I*." So start listening to the words that you and your colleagues say. Tape-record and listen to a couple of meetings; if they are nearly all about "me, myself, and I" and "us versus them," it might be time to start changing the way you talk—it can help keep your inner jerk in check.

Second, adopt a frame that turns your attention to ways in which you are no better or worse than other people. Don't focus on all the big and little ways that you are superior (provoking arrogance and negative opinions of others) or inferior (provoking envy and hostility). Think of all the ways that fellow human beings are just like you, such as the needs that we all have for love, comfort, happiness, and respect. I realized the power of this frame when an in-home closet designer named Wendy spent several hours at my house to design a new storage system. When I asked about her about her business, she said that the key to designing a good closet and to having interesting and respectful interactions with clients was to focus on the ways in which all people are alike. "We are all the same" was Wendy's mantra.

Wendy made her point with an extreme comparison. She explained that she approached me and my closet in exactly the same way as her last client—a sadomasochist who needed room to hang up his whips and chains. Wendy listened to him, measured his stuff, and thought about what he needed. And she added that, really, my needs—and my closet—"weren't much different than his" (even though I had no whips and chains) because, once you get past the surface, we are "all the same" in most ways. There are, of course, many ways in which people differ. There are also good reasons for celebrating such differences and rewarding people based on different skills and performance levels. Yet I think that Wendy's philosophy and framing are constructive for reminding us of our common humanity, which helps us see and treat other people in ways we would like to be treated.

Finally, if you read or watch TV programs about business or sports, you often see the world framed as a place where everyone wants "more more more for me me me," every minute in every way. The old bumper sticker sums it up: "Whoever dies with the most toys wins." The potent but usually unstated message is that we are all trapped in a lifelong contest where people can never get enough money, prestige, victories, cool stuff, beauty, or sex—and that we do and should want more goodies than everyone else.

This attitude fuels a quest for constant improvement that has a big upside, leading to everything from more beautiful athletic and artistic performances to more elegant and functional products to better surgical procedures and medicines to more effective and humane organizations. Yet when taken too far, this blend of constant dissatisfaction, unquenchable desires, and overbearing competitiveness can damage your mental health. It can lead you to treat those "below" you as inferior creatures who are worthy of your disdain and people "above" you who have more stuff and status as objects of envy and jealousy.

Again, a bit of framing can help. Tell yourself, "I have enough." Certainly, some people need more than they have, as many people on earth still need a safe place to live, enough good food to eat, and other necessities. But too many of us are never satisfied and feel constantly slighted, even though—by objective standards—we have all we need to live a good life. I got this idea from a lovely little poem that Kurt Vonnegut published in the *New Yorker* called "Joe Heller," which was about the author of the renowned World War II novel *Catch-22*. The poem describes a party that Heller and Vonnegut attended at a billionaire's house. Heller remarks to Vonnegut that he has something that the billionaire can never have—"the knowledge that I've got enough." These wise words provide a frame that can help you to be at peace with yourself and to treat those around you with affection and respect.

JOE HELLER

True story, Word of Honor:
Joseph Heller, an important and funny writer
now dead,
and I were at a party given by a billionaire
on Shelter Island.
I said, "Joe, how does it make you feel
to know that our host only yesterday
may have made more money
than your novel *Catch-22*
has earned in its entire history?"
And Joe said, "I've got something he can never have."
And I said, "What on earth could that be, Joe?"
And Joe said, "The knowledge that I've got enough."
Not bad! Rest in peace!

—Kurt Vonnegut
The New Yorker, May 16, 2005

SEE YOURSELF AS OTHERS DO

I've been careful to define assholes in terms of their effects on others. Recall the first of the two "asshole detector" tests that I introduced early in the book: *After talk-*

*ing to the alleged asshole, does the "target" feel oppressed, humili-
ated, de-energized, or belittled by the person? In particular, does he
or she feel worse about him or herself?* This test means that
whether or not you think you are an asshole is less important than what other people think. And hundreds of
studies by psychologists show that nearly all human beings travel through life with distorted, and often inflated,
beliefs about how they treat, affect, and are seen by others. If you want to confront the hard facts about yourself
rather than wallowing in your protective delusions, try
contrasting what you believe about yourself with how
others see you.

Work by executive coaches Kate Ludeman and Eddie
Erlandson on alpha males shows how this ought to be
done. These coaches emphasize that alpha males have
upsides too, including the ability to act decisively and
produce results, so it isn't fair to simply label them as
assholes. As we've seen, however, there are striking similarities. Ludeman and Erlandson learned that when they
want to change an alpha male's destructive behavior,
they first collect information about how he is viewed by
superiors, peers, and subordinates: for one client, they
collected fifty pages of information about his actions
from thirty-five different people, and then summarized it
for him in a one-page chart. Ludeman and Erlandson say
that although they often get defensive at first, many
alpha males find themselves unable to argue with such
overwhelming evidence, and it motivates them to
change.

As these coaches reported in *Harvard Business Review*, among their most famous clients are Michael Dell (founder and chairman of computer giant Dell) and Kevin Rollins (current Dell CEO). Michael Dell's subordinates saw him as remote, impatient, and unappreciative. People who worked with Rollins saw him as overly critical, opinionated, and a poor listener because he was so quick to jump in with his own suggestion and ignore their ideas. Neither Dell nor Rollins realized how much fear and frustration they were breeding in the company.

To their credit, both have worked hard to change their negative behavior, and they now monitor their progress with regular 360-degree evaluations. Dell and Rollins also used serious humor to help contain what I would call their inner jerks. Rollins, for example, got himself a Curious George stuffed animal to remind himself "to be more inquiring and open to other people's ideas." They also made more systematic changes in company practices, including working with human resources to change the profile of the ideal Dell general manager to reflect an increased emphasis on listening to people and treating them with respect. And after Dell and Rollins began talking openly about their weaknesses, it gave other senior executives "permission" to talk about their own nastiness and insensitivity, and gave their colleagues permission to "call them" on bad behavior. As one general manager put it, "After someone discloses that he periodically lobs grenades into meetings but intends to stop, we all have permission to call him on it. And we do."

FACE YOUR PAST

I've focused on how people can avoid catching and spreading asshole poisoning regardless of their particular inner demons. I've done so because too much existing advice about managing jerks, bullies, and abusive supervisors—including advice on how they ought to manage themselves—places too much weight on personalities. And it doesn't place enough weight on how asshole poisoning is something that almost anyone can catch. Despite claims in some books that "a leopard does not change its spots" and "born a jerk, die a jerk," a massive body of psychological research shows that, at best, personality has only moderate effects on what people do in different situations. I've also avoided focusing too much on personal traits because, compared to the time and effort it takes to change your personality or someone else's, you get more bang for the buck by doing (or teaching others to do) straightforward things like picking the place you work, walking out of a bad place, avoiding nasty people, changing your "frame," and "testing" how other people see you (and making adjustments as a result). Such steps aren't simple or painless. But they are a lot easier—and more likely to succeed—than transforming the personality that you were born with or that was ingrained in you as a child.

This doesn't mean that personality doesn't matter. Researchers have uncovered and labeled thousands of personality characteristics. And hundreds of these traits can make a person more or less prone to act like an asshole.

Examples include anxiety, aggression, dominance, emotional stability, primal trauma, passive-aggression, type A behavior, need for control, neuroticism, narcissism, paranoia, tolerance, trust, warmth, and on and on and on. It is impossible to drag you through an "asshole proneness analysis" of every known personality and background measure in this little book. But there is one big lesson that you ought to know, an old saying in psychology that is backed by reams of evidence: *The best predictor of future behavior is past behavior.* This simple truth means that facing the facts about your dark past—just as alcoholics and other addicts do in their treatment—can be a powerful way to assess and start changing your "asshole proneness."

Ask yourself whether you were a bully in school. There are hundreds of studies of bullying in schools, of children who repeatedly oppress and humiliate their classmates. Researcher Dan Olweus has done particularly rigorous studies in Norway, surveying more than 130,000 students and doing long-term follow-up studies of both bullies and their victims. His research shows that about 7% of Norwegian children are bullies and about 9% are victims. This research further shows that it is possible to predict which kids will become bullies, typically those who were raised by cold or aggressive parents, those whose parents let them get away with aggression, and those who had a history of "an active and hotheaded temperament" before starting school. There isn't any systematic research showing that schoolyard bullies become workplace bullies, but Olweus's research shows that such nastiness persists into

adulthood, as approximately 60% of boys who were identified as bullies in grades six through nine were convicted
of at least one crime by the time they were twenty-four
years old (compared to only 10% of kids who weren't bullies). These findings are dramatic enough that it isn't much
of a stretch to assume that if you were a bully in school,
you will be more prone to taunting, teasing, threatening,
and even doing physical harm to your coworkers.

Facing the facts about your past behavior can help you
assess your "risk" of acting like an asshole in the future.
But there is also intriguing research by anthropologists,
historians, and psychologists suggesting that the culture
you were raised in can amplify your risk, especially if you
grew up in an aggressive and violence-prone country, region, or neighborhood. To illustrate, following research at
the University of Michigan by Dov Cohen and his colleagues, you might have been raised in a "culture of
honor," a region or group "in which even small disputes
become contests for reputation and social status." Anthropological research shows that these are cultures where
men gain and sustain status by being known as someone
who "can't be pushed around" and "who won't take any
shit." American examples cited by Cohen and his colleagues include the old "cowboy" western and southern
United States. These were both once unruly and unstable
places where law enforcement was largely absent and
where one's wealth and social standing could easily be
wrested away by others—and even though that has
changed in many parts of the West and South, the culture

of honor persists to this day. People raised in these cultures are especially polite and considerate in most interactions, in part because they want to avoid threatening the honor of others (and the fight it provokes)—even long after they have moved to another part of the country. Once they are affronted, men raised in these places often feel obligated to lash back and protect what is theirs, especially their right to be treated with respect or "honor."

Experiments by Cohen and his colleagues that were published in the *Journal of Personality and Social Psychology* show that for men raised in the southern United States, the culture of honor continues to have measurable and strong effects even after they have moved to the northern United States In this 1996 study at the University of Michigan, subjects (half southerners and half northerners) passed a stooge who "accidentally" bumped into him and called him an asshole. There were big differences between how the northerners and southerners reacted: 65% of the northerners were amused by the bump and insult, and only 35% got angry; only 15% of the insulted southerners were amused, and 85% got angry. Not only that, a second study showed that southerners had strong physiological reactions to being bumped, especially substantial increases in cortisol (a hormone associated with high levels of stress and anxiety), as well as some signs of increased testosterone levels. Yet northerners showed no signs of physiological reaction to the bump and insult.

The lesson from these experiments, plus a host of other studies, is that if you were raised as a southerner—or perhaps a cowboy—you will likely be more polite than your colleagues most of the time, but if you run into an even mildly insulting asshole, you are prone to lash out and risk fueling a cycle of asshole poisoning.

The Upshot: Asshole, Know Thyself

Dave Sanford just graduated from Stanford in 2006. Dave is one of my favorite students of all time, in part because he has so much self-awareness (he is also brilliant and charming). When I told Dave about this book, he told me how, when he first came to Stanford as a freshman, some classmates thought that he was a jerk because they weren't accustomed to his sense of humor, especially his tendency to look completely serious even when he was joking. Dave made a big effort to understand how other people experienced him and to stop doing things that provoked people who didn't know him well to mislabel him as a jerk. Dave showed me a button (see picture) that his brother gave him to help with this crusade that said, "Admitting you're an asshole is the first step." That button captures much of what this chapter is about: to keep your inner asshole from getting out, you need to be aware of places and people that will turn you into an asshole. You have to be aware of how seeing life as a bitter winner-takes-all contest can turn you into an instant jerk, and of how others see you even if it doesn't reflect your true intentions (like Dave, you might learn how to stop people from mislabeling you as a

jerk). The upshot is: *to avoid acting like or becoming a known ass-hole, know thyself.*

I've coached youth sports a bit over the years. I wish I had one of these buttons to give out to those obnoxious parents who bellow out highly inappropriate critiques, insults, and unwanted advice from the sidelines—upsetting the kids and making the game into a horrid experience for everyone involved. At their worst, these overbearing sports parents are among the most clueless and craziest assholes I've ever encountered. Last year, I was assistant soccer coach for a team of nine-year-old girls. An ugly episode happened when one of "our" parents became so upset at the referee's call that he ran onto the field in the middle of the game to berate the referee. When I asked the parent to get off the field, explaining that he was violating both the letter and the spirit of the league rules, he got so mad—his veins were popping, and he started glaring at me and screaming insults—that I thought he was going to punch me.

Thinking back on that incident and others like it, perhaps—building on the current soccer rules for unsportsmanlike conduct by players—the rules for youth sports ought to be modified so that referees can award a "yellow card" to, say, suspend a nasty parent from the sidelines of a game for ten minutes and a "red card" to expel persistently or excessively vile parents for the entire game. Perhaps both the message and the public humiliation could help some of these parents gain badly needed self-awareness—and cleanse the kids' games of these horrible role models.

I've already talked about ways to achieve such self-knowledge and self-control, arguing that you ought to look at the people around you and into your past to assess—and perhaps reduce—your risk of spreading and catching such poison. You can also take a more direct approach to self-knowledge and do a personal "asshole audit."

If you are interested in "real-time" information, look into a device invented by Anmol Madan and his colleagues at the MIT Media Lab. His gizmo is called the Jerk-O-Meter, and people can use it as an asshole detector to help them realize when they are being nasty or insensitive. The Jerk-O-Meter attaches to your phone and uses electronic speech analysis to provide instant feedback to the person speaking on factors including stress, empathy, and "overall jerk factor." These MIT researchers claim: "The mathematical models for the Jerk-O-Meter were derived from several research studies at the Media Lab. These studies evaluated how a person's speaking style could reflect his or her interest in a conversation, in going out on a date, or perhaps even in buying a particular product. Our results show that a person's speaking style and 'tone of voice' can predict objective outcomes (e.g., interest in a conversation or in going out on a date) with 75–85% accuracy."

THE MIT JERK-O-METER

I like the Jerk-O-Meter because it measures how people are acting *in the moment.* After all, one of the main ideas in this book is that the no asshole rule is meaningless— regardless of what you say, what policies you enact, and the best of intentions—unless you treat the person *right in front of you, right now, in the right way.*

Unfortunately, the Jerk-O-Meter isn't available in stores. And even if it ever is, it doesn't measure everything you do (only voice tone) and doesn't assess how others react to you. So I've also developed a little self-test to help you figure out if you are a certified asshole. The test is inspired by the research and ideas here, although it has not been validated by rigorous scientific studies. But you might find it to be a useful tool for launching your personal asshole audit.

Start out by completing the twenty-four true/false questions ("Self-Test: Are You a Certified Asshole?" on p.124–6) about your gut reactions to people, how you treat others, and how others react to you. Bear in mind that this is just an impromptu test, but take a moment to see how you score. You might be surprised!

If you want even better evidence, follow the lead of Dell executives and find out what other people think about you. Just take the list of questions and change "you" to your name. So, if your name is Chris, the first statement would be "Chris feels surrounded by incompetent idiots— and he can't help letting them know the truth every now and then." Beware that if you can't protect the anonymity of people who complete the survey about you, be suspicious if they don't rate you as an asshole. If you are a known jerk, they will fear your wrath and revenge. If your audit is done right, and all signs are that you are prone to act like a jerk, take another look at the ideas in this chapter. And remember that just because you are an asshole and have the courage to admit it doesn't mean that you are qualified to help yourself, other nasty colleagues, or your organization eradicate this problem. As my son Tyler likes to say, "Just because you suffer from an affliction does not mean that you are an expert on it."

Taken together, this chapter and the last provide a one-two punch that can help you enforce the no asshole rule. If you manage your organization so that the no asshole rule reigns *and* manage yourself to avoid catching and spreading asshole poisoning, you can fuel a virtuous cycle that can help sustain a civilized workplace. Unfortunately, life isn't always so sweet. There are times when people can't avoid taking a job in Jerk City or when, once they do, they become trapped (or feel trapped). The next chapter offers ideas about how to survive in a place where every workday feels like a walk down Asshole Avenue.

SELF-TEST: ARE YOU A CERTIFIED ASSHOLE?

Signs That Your Inner Jerk Is Rearing Its Ugly Head

Instructions: indicate whether each statement is a true (T) or false (F) description of your typical feelings and interactions with the people at your workplace.

What Are Your Gut Reactions to People?

____ 1. You feel surrounded by incompetent idiots—and you can't help letting them know the truth every now and then.

____ 2. You were a nice person until you started working with the current bunch of creeps.

____ 3. You don't trust the people around you, and they don't trust you.

____ 4. You see your coworkers as competitors.

____ 5. You believe that one of the best ways to "climb the ladder" is to push other people down or out of the way.

____ 6. You secretly enjoy watching other people suffer and squirm.

____ 7. You are often jealous of your colleagues and find it difficult to be genuinely pleased for them when they do well.

____ 8. You have a small list of close friends and a long list of enemies, and you are equally proud of both lists.

How Do You Treat Other People?

____ 9. You sometimes just can't contain your contempt toward the losers and jerks at your workplace.

___ 10. You find it useful to glare at, insult, and even occasionally holler at some of the idiots at your workplace—otherwise, they never seem to shape up.

___ 11. You take credit for the accomplishments of your team—why not? They would be nowhere without you.

___ 12. You enjoy lobbing "innocent" comments into meetings that serve no purpose other than to humiliate or cause discomfort to the person on the receiving end.

___ 13. You are quick to point out others' mistakes.

___ 14. You don't make mistakes. When something goes wrong, you always find some idiot to blame.

___ 15. You constantly interrupt people because, after all, what you have to say is more important.

___ 16. You are constantly buttering up your boss and other powerful people, and you expect the same treatment from your underlings.

___ 17. Your jokes and teasing can get a bit nasty at times, but you have to admit that they are pretty funny.

___ 18. You love your immediate team and they love you, but you are all at constant warfare with the rest of the organization. You treat everyone else like crap because, after all, if you're not on my team, you either don't matter or are the enemy.

How Do People React to You?

___ 19. You notice that people seem to avoid eye contact when they talk to you—and they often become very nervous.

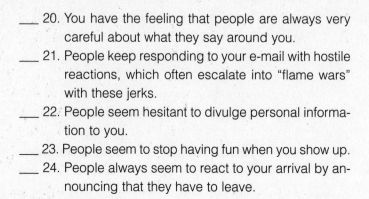

___ 20. You have the feeling that people are always very careful about what they say around you.

___ 21. People keep responding to your e-mail with hostile reactions, which often escalate into "flame wars" with these jerks.

___ 22. People seem hesitant to divulge personal information to you.

___ 23. People seem to stop having fun when you show up.

___ 24. People always seem to react to your arrival by announcing that they have to leave.

Scoring the test: add up the number of statements that you marked as true. This isn't a scientifically validated test, but in my opinion:

0–5 true: you don't sound like a certified asshole, unless you are fooling yourself.

5–15 true: You sound like a borderline certified asshole; perhaps the time has come to start changing your behavior before it gets worse.

15 or more true: You sound like a full-blown certified asshole to me; get help immediately. But please, don't come to me for help, as I would rather not meet you.

Chapter 5

When Assholes Reign: Tips for Surviving Nasty People and Workplaces

Millions of people feel trapped in places where "the pro asshole rule" rather than the no asshole rule prevails. Employees who face and witness constant bullying do leave their jobs at higher rates than in civilized places.

Researchers Charlotte Rayner and Loraleigh Keashly estimate that 25% of victims and 20% of witnesses of bullying leave their jobs, compared to a typical rate of about 5%. But these numbers also show that most of the afflicted hunker down and take it. Many people are stuck in vile workplaces for financial reasons—they have no escape route to another job, at least to one that pays as well. Even good jobs in civilized places involve run-ins with nasty people, especially service jobs. JetBlue flight attendants, 7-Eleven clerks, Starbucks baristas, Disneyland cast members, business school professors, and McKinsey consultants all have told me that sometimes they "just have to take it" from demeaning customers.

And even people who are planning to escape a wicked workplace may choose to endure weeks or months of abuse before walking out. A *Harvard Business Review* reader wrote to me that his software company had "jerks in management that crush their employees" and made them feel "worthless," so the best programmers kept leaving, but only after lining up another job. People may also tolerate abuse for a while because they promised to finish a project, are holding out for a year-end bonus, or are waiting for stock options or a retirement plan to vest. Yet whether you are a "short-timer" or face a long sentence embedded with a bumper crop of assholes, there are ways to make the best of a bad situation.

Consider the strategy that one Silicon Valley executive used to survive her mean-spirited colleagues. Let's call her Ruth to protect the innocent as well as the guilty. Earlier in her career, Ruth became tangled in a nasty political battle with "a slew of assholes" who routinely put her down, interrupted her, and glared at her in meetings. They repeatedly criticized what she did and shot down her solutions, while offering few constructive ideas of their own. They proposed tough solutions (such as firing poor performers) and then lacked the courage to implement their macho talk—leaving her to do their dirty work.

These pompous table pounders also repeatedly instructed Ruth to take actions and then criticized her for doing *exactly* what they asked. Ruth tried to fight back and was beaten down. Although she weathered the storm and kept her position, she emerged with her confidence eroded and was physically and emotionally exhausted. Ruth lost weight and had a hard time sleeping for months after the abuse she suffered at the hands of these jerks.

Three years later, a similar dynamic reared its ugly head again, with the same creeps using the same dirty tricks. This time, Ruth went in with her eyes open, determined to get through it all without letting them "get" to her. Ruth's coping strategy was inspired by advice she had gotten as a teenager from a river rafting guide: If you fall out of the boat in rapids, don't try to fight it; just rely on your life vest and float with your feet out in front of you. That way, if you are thrown up against rocks, you can use your feet to push off, and you will protect your head and conserve your energy. As it turned out, Ruth had fallen overboard, in a stretch of the American River in California known as Satan's Cesspool. The guide's advice worked perfectly: after an amazing trip through the rapids, with her feet out in front of her, Ruth came to a smooth stretch of river and swam over to the boat, which was waiting for her by a gentle beach.

Ruth remembered this strategy when she was trapped in a different kind of cesspool: a meeting—the first of several—where she and a few others were subjected to personal attacks, dirty looks, and excessive blame. The asshole contagion spread like wildfire, even infecting people who were usually kind and sensible. Ruth stretched out her feet in front of her under the table, and then the river rafting image came to her. She told herself, "I just got thrown out of the boat by these assholes," and she realized, "I know how to survive."

Instead of seeing herself as a victim, Ruth started to feel strong. She realized that if she didn't panic and just "floated with her feet out in front," she would come out of the mess in one piece and with her energy intact for whatever lay ahead. And that is exactly what happened. After that meeting, she shared her strategy with a fellow executive who was also being bad-mouthed and bullied—and it worked for that executive, too. Both "targets" believed that it was effective because, instead of feeling like wimps for floating along, it felt like they were making a choice to bounce off the boulders that these jerks were flinging in their paths. It became empowering, and they sent regular reminders to each other to "just stay feet first." Both made it through this ordeal with their energy and confidence intact. Rather than lowering themselves to catching and flinging back the venom that spewed out of these creeps, they remained calm and helped others weather the storm as well. They found subtle ways to "out" the most toxic of these assholes, to expose the damage that they had done to their victims and to the company. And Ruth and her colleagues emerged from the ordeal with the energy and confidence to seek employment elsewhere.

Ruth's "Satan's Cesspool Strategy" contains two key ingredients that help people keep their mental and physical health intact—and get their jobs done—even though they are surrounded by a pack of brutal bullies. First, Ruth learned to *reframe* the nastiness that she faced in ways that helped her become emotionally detached from the assholes—even downright indifferent to what was happening. Second, Ruth didn't struggle against larger forces that she couldn't control. She focused instead on small ways to gain tidbits of control, including helping fellow victims cope with the jerks by teaching the victims her strategy, giving them emotional support, and concentrating on helping the good people in the company. Ruth also picked small battles she could win and took small steps to undermine the worst of her tormentors. Rather than fighting big wars that she was destined to lose and would leave her exhausted and debased like the first time this happened, Ruth was wise enough this time to *look for small wins* to sustain her confidence and a sense of control.

Reframing: Change How You See Things

Psychologists have found that if you can't escape a source of stress, changing your mind-set about what is happening to you, or reframing, can help reduce the damage done to you. Some useful reframing tricks include avoiding self-blame, hoping for the best but expecting the worst, and, my favorite, developing indifference and emotional detachment. Learning when and how to simply not give a damn isn't the kind of advice you hear in most business books, but it can help you make the best of a lousy situation.

Martin Seligman's research on "learned optimism" shows that when people view difficulties as temporary and not their fault, and as something that will not pervade and ruin the rest of their lives, this frame protects their mental and physical health and enhances their resilience. Noreen Tehrani is a counseling psychologist in the United Kingdom who has extensive experience working with victims of workplace bullying. Tehrani says that when she debriefs victims, common "irrational" thoughts include "I will never get over this," "I must have done something wrong for this to happen to me," and "Everyone hates me."

Tehrani uses cognitive behavioral therapy (based on Seligman's work) to help victims view such irrational beliefs as hypotheses rather than facts and develop a different, and more optimistic frame for interpreting encounters with bullies. Ruth's coping strategy had elements of Tehrani's approach. Think about the differences between how Ruth framed her experience with the assholes during her first versus her second ordeal. Ruth emphasized to me, "The second time, I realized it wasn't my fault and I wasn't going to blame myself." And her "Satan's Cesspool Strategy" helped her frame her encounters with the gang of assholes as part of a temporary ordeal that she would float through, that she would come out of in one piece.

Disney uses a related strategy to train employees (called cast members) in their theme parks to deal with irate guests. The added twist is that corporate trainers teach new cast members to avoiding blaming either themselves or their abusive guests. Years ago, a former student

of mine took copious notes during her new employee orientation classes at Disney University. Her instructors emphasized that although 99% of guests are nice, the real test
is when you are encircled by an angry family of eight who
are all hollering at you about all the things that have gone
wrong. The new cast members were instructed to avoiding getting angry at or blaming the nasty guests. They
were asked to imagine all the awful experiences the family suffered that whipped them into such a hostile state
(e.g., to imagine that their car broke down or they just got
soaked in the rain) and to not take their anger personally
(as it isn't your fault).

Cast members were also reminded to see the abuse as
something that wouldn't last long (because most other
guests are nice) and that it "didn't need to ruin your day"
because, if they "just keep smiling" and "treat people as
VIPs," it will create friendly interactions with other guests,
and might even turn the family that is hollering at you
right now into nicer people. The percentage of nasty people in Ruth's company was higher than at a Disney theme
park, but the optimistic style she used has much in common with how Disney cast members frame bouts with
bombastic guests.

Hope for the Best; Expect the Worst

As Seligman's research and Ruth's experience show, framing demeaning encounters in an optimistic light can help
sustain your physical and mental health. Yet, especially if

you are subjected to mean-spirited people for long stretches, unbridled optimism can be dangerous to your spirit and esteem. Unwavering hope that all those hard-core jerks are going to be transformed into nice people is a recipe for one reliable disappointment after another. If you expect that, one beautiful day, all those assholes will suddenly apologize to you, begin begging for your for-giveness, or at least start treating you with respect, you are setting yourself up for disappointment and frustration.

Psychologists who study emotions propose that happi-ness reflects the difference between what you expect ver-sus what you actually get in life—so if you keep expecting good things to happen, but they never do or take a turn for the worse, you will suffer constant unhappiness. The trick, as we saw from Ruth's example, is not to expect that the jerks will change their behavior. Keep your expecta-tions for their behavior low, but continue to believe that you will be fine after the ordeal is over. That way, you won't be surprised or upset by your colleagues' relentless nastiness. And if they do show you unexpected moments of kindness, you can enjoy the pleasant surprise without suffering disappointment when they return to their wicked ways.

The effectiveness (and dangers) of lowering your ex-pectations and accepting that your boss is an abusive jerk are illustrated by an interview in *Gig* with a film develop-ment assistant identified as Jerrold Thomas. His job was to read and evaluate scripts (and do anything else required) for a hotheaded Hollywood producer, who was called

Brad in the interview. Brad expected Jerrold to be at work from 6:30 A.M. to 11:00 P.M., routinely called him at 3:00 A.M. with additional chores, and threw a "fit" when an answering machine (rather than Jerrold) picked up calls. In Jerrold's interview in *Gig*, he said the job was "constant stress" and that Brad "bullies me and calls me stupid and stuff." Jerrold once interrupted a "closed-door meeting" with a director (to deliver a pack of cigarettes that Brad ordered him to get for the director); Brad got so mad that he came out and started "strangling me" and yelling, "Are you stupid?" When Jerrold explained that he was just following Brad's orders, Brad reacted by "whaling on me with both fists."

One way that Jerrold survived such abuse was by lowering his expectations. As he put it, "I understand. I mean, of course, that I wish that Brad would be a little nicer to his underlings and not yell. But I also understand that's not a realistic wish, because there is too much money at stake for everybody to act like fucking saints." Jerrold also endured the abuse by taking delight in the moments when Brad was nice to him and showed respect for his opinion, and Jerrold looked to the future, to what he might gain from surviving the ordeal. Jerrold hoped that Brad would help him land his own lucrative deals in the future. Jerrold also admitted that success may not happen for him and half-joked, "I'll probably be here until I have some kind of nervous breakdown."

Jerrold's story shows how having low expectations for an asshole boss, focusing on the good things, and being optimistic about how it will all end can help someone endure a horrible situation. For better and worse, it helped him endure a horrible situation that most sensible people before him *had* left—Brad had burned through ten assistants in four months before Jerrold arrived.

Develop Indifference and Emotional Detachment

Passion is an overrated virtue in organizational life, and indifference is an underrated virtue. This conclusion clashes with most business books, which ballyhoo the magical powers of exuding deep and authentic passion about your work, organization, colleagues, and customers. Management guru Tom Peters has been talking about the importance of pride and enthusiasm for your workplace and your clients for more than twenty years. Former AES CEO Dennis Bakke advocates building workplaces where people experience joy and fun at work and are emotionally fulfilled at all times. Jim Collins's blockbuster *Good to Great* urges leaders to give seats on "the bus" only to "A level people" who are passionate enough to give "A+ level" efforts. And we saw in chapter 3 how Southwest Airlines doesn't just try to avoid hiring jerks; they hire and brainwash people to exude a zeal for their coworkers, customers, and company.

All this talk about passion, commitment, and identification with an organization is absolutely correct *if* you are in a good job and are treated with dignity and respect. But it is hypocritical nonsense to the millions of people who are trapped in jobs and companies where they feel oppressed and humiliated—where their goal is to survive with their health and self-esteem intact and provide for their families, not to do great things for a company that treats them like dirt. Organizations that are filled with employees who don't give a damn about their jobs will suffer poor performance, but in my book, if they routinely demean employees, they get what they deserve.

When organizational life takes this ugly turn, linking your self-worth to how people treat you and putting all your effort and emotional energy into your workplace is a path to exploitation and self-destruction. Self-preservation sometimes requires the opposite response: learn to feel and practice *indifference and emotional detachment.* When your job feels like a prolonged personal insult, focus on just going through the motions, on caring as little as possible about the jerks around you, and think about something more pleasant as often as you can—just get through each day until something changes at your job or something better comes along. We all face bad situations that we must endure. None of us has complete mastery over our surroundings, and we all get stuck with oppressive jerks whom we can't change. There are times when the best thing for your mental health is to not give a damn about your job, company, and, especially, all those nasty people. As Walt Whitman said, "Dismiss whatever insults your soul." I think that is a lovely, compact summary of the virtues of developing indifference to demeaning jerks in the workplace, or anywhere else for that matter.

Some researchers have suggested that "detached concern" can help employees avoid the "burnout" that results from constant exposure to other people's problems. Christina Maslach defines detached concern as "the medical profession's ideal of blending compassion with emotional distance . . . and a more detached objectivity." Yet Maslach has found that people in medicine and other helping professions have trouble sustaining this balance: either people genuinely care about others (and risk burnout), or they put on an act (often a bad act) because, after all, they don't really care. The implication is that you can feel either attached concern or detached indifference, but caring and passion without emotional attachment is difficult or impossible.

If you can't bring yourself to care about good colleagues, clients, and organizations, it is a sign that you need a break, to learn a new skill, or perhaps to move to a different job. But detached indifference, simply not giving a damn, might be the best that you can do to survive a workplace that subjects you to relentless humiliation. Think about what Ruth did as she imagined herself floating through the rapids, feet first, as her colleagues heaped on the abuse. Ruth was physically sitting at the table. In her mind, however, she wasn't attached to her nasty and demeaning colleagues, their opinions didn't affect her self-worth, their vile expressions and words weren't touching her soul, and she was in a different and better world.

Look for Small Wins

The ability to gain control over little, seemingly trivial things is a hallmark of people who survive horrible and uncontrollable events—including natural disasters or being a castaway, a hostage, or a prisoner of war. Vice Admiral James Stockdale was held prisoner by the North Vietnamese from 1965 to 1973. He found a common thread among prisoners like him who survived the ordeal: "We discovered that when one is alone in a cell and sees the door open only once or twice a day for a bowl of soup, he realizes that after a period of isolation and darkness, he has to build some sort of ritual into his life if he wants to avoid becoming an animal. . . . For most of us, ritual was built around prayer, exercise, and clandestine communication." Stockdale and other prisoners survived by finding hundreds of tiny actions they could take each day to take a modicum of control over their lives—like saying a prayer, doing some push-ups, or trying to develop new ways to get a secret message to other prisoners.

Rigorous research confirms that the feeling of control— perceiving that you have the power to shape even small aspects of your fate—can have a huge impact on human well-being. Consider a compelling study by Ellen Langer and Judith Rodin with elderly patients in nursing homes.

One group of patients attended a lecture about all the things that the staff could do for them; they were given a houseplant and told the staff would care for it, and they were told which night to attend movies. Patients in the other (quite similar) groups from the same nursing homes were given a "pep talk" about the importance of taking control over their lives, asked to take care of the new houseplant in their rooms, and given choices about which nights to attend movies, when they had meals, when their phones rang, and how their furniture was arranged. These small differences had big effects. Not only did those patients with greater control engage in more recreational activities and have more positive attitudes toward life in general, an eighteen-month follow-up found that they had a 50% lower death rate.

Along similar lines, psychologist Karl Weick contends that aiming for "small wins" is often a more comforting and ultimately effective strategy than aiming for "big wins." Weick shows that trying to solve a big problem all at once can be so daunting and upsetting that it causes people to feel anxious and powerless in the face of an impossible challenge. The advantage of taking small actions is that they bring about noticeable and typically successful changes. As we saw with the tiny changes made by Vice Admiral Stockdale and the nursing home patients, *the feeling that one is in control can reduce feelings of hopelessness and helplessness.*

Weick also argues that most big problems can be solved only one small step at a time. There are no instant, massive, magic solutions to ending world hunger or cleaning up the environment, but progress can be made if many people take many small, positive steps in the right direction. Another advantage is that while efforts to win a big victory may provoke a more powerful opponent to spring into action against you, an opponent may think it is too much trouble to undermine or overturn any given tiny victory, or may not even notice that it has happened. Yet, over time, a series of small wins may add up to a big win against that opponent.

The implication for surviving a workplace where assholes abound is that if you can't escape completely, start looking for small ways to seize bits of control. Try to find little steps you can take to reduce your exposure to their venom. Build pockets of safety and support, as the act of helping others alone is good for your mental health. If you can't win the big war against the creeps, start looking for small battles that you can win, as the sense of control you gain will sustain your spirit. And if one minor victory after another begins to pile up, who knows—you might start a movement in your organization where the pro asshole rule is slowly but surely replaced by the no asshole rule.

Limit Your Exposure

This tactic dampens the damage that assholes do in two ways. First, by limiting how often and intensely you face their dirty looks and demeaning words, you suffer less direct damage. Second, as we've seen, *anything* that gains you even tiny bits of control can protect your sense of self, spirit, and physical health. My first suggestion is to find places and times where and when you can hide from your tormentors. Meet with them as rarely as possible. Schedule meetings that will be short—in particular, recent research suggests that you might schedule meetings in rooms or places with no chairs. An experiment by Allen C. Bluedorn and his colleagues at the University of Missouri–Columbia compared the decisions made by fifty-six groups where members *stood up* during short (ten- to twenty-minute) meetings to those of fifty-five groups where members *sat down* during such meetings. Stand-up groups took 34% less time to make the assigned decision, and the quality of their decisions was just as good as those made by sit-down groups.

In addition to the time you can save your organization, if you are scheduling a meeting with known assholes, finding a place with no chairs can apparently cut your exposure time by 34%. A related implication is that setting aside a few conference rooms with "stand-up tables" and no chairs can help people in your company with both time management and asshole management—and save some money on chairs.

You can also use information technologies to help buffer you from a jerk or a bunch of jerks. For example, in addition to "Satan's Cesspool Strategy," described at the start of this chapter, Ruth buffered herself from that swarm of assholes by attending a couple of meetings via a telephone conference call rather than in person. That way, she didn't have to see the nasty looks on their faces, she found it easier to detach emotionally, and there were times when she blanked out a jerk that was making her stomach turn by hitting the mute button, tuning out her colleagues' nastiness, and devoting her attention to helping the good people in the company instead. Be warned, however, that when groups work mostly through e-mail or conference calls (rather than face-to-face), they tend to fight more and trust each other less. Apparently, this happens because people don't get the complete picture that comes with "being there," as e-mail and phone calls provide little information about the demands that people face and the physical setting they work in, and can't convey things like the facial expressions, verbal intonations, posture, and "group mood." So group members develop incomplete, and often overly negative, opinions of one another.

My Stanford colleagues Pamela Hinds and Diane Bailey show that conflict—especially "disagreements characterized by anger and hostility"—is more likely and trust is lower when groups do work that is "mediated" by information technologies than in face-to-face meetings. If you are in a group that works mostly via the Web and the phone, and the group seems like a bunch of assholes, *the technology may be fueling the problem rather than simply protecting you from it*—so you might spend time meeting in person to understand the pressures people face and develop greater trust. Yet you might be like Ruth and already have had extensive experience in face-to-face meetings where people proved they are assholes. If so, then e-mail, telephone conferences, and the almighty mute button might help protect you from the full sting of their wrath.

Build Pockets of Safety, Support, and Sanity

Find and build some pockets where you can hide from assholes and hang out with decent people. Doing so can reduce your exposure to jerks, give you a breather, and provide a bit of control over when and how these creeps do their dirty work to you. These pockets can be buildings or rooms. For example, the nurses that Daniel Denison and I studied felt besieged by surgeons who were insensitive and demeaning, especially the infamous "Dr. Gooser," who we witnessed chasing, teasing, and grabbing the female nurses. They took refuge in the nurse's lounge, where doctors weren't allowed to tread. It was a safe place to tell stories, complain, and give and receive emotional support; the drop in tension that most nurses experienced the second they entered the lounge was palpable.

Another way to find a safe pocket is to join or form a secret social network of victims. A group of secretaries in a university formed a prayer group that met regularly for several months to help shorten the tenure of their cold-hearted and clueless dean. They prayed that something would happen to him that was not too bad, but bad enough to hasten his departure! (Alas, their efforts were not successful; as of this writing, he still has the job.) Similarly, an executive's wife wrote to me how her husband struggled to survive his abusive CEO: "The senior people just below him all huddle together in one another's offices trying to give one another support, but they're all very conscious of the fact that any one of them could decide to throw in the towel and then the stress would be redistributed on those who are left." In some organizations where bullies rule the roost, their victims are so afraid of reprisals that networks and conversations among victims are treated as secret and forbidden acts—but as worth the risk because the stress is severe.

These pockets can be found in even tiny moments, such as during brief interactions with supportive customers or clients. A few months ago, I was standing in line at a Longs drugstore in Moraga, California. Our cashier was a teenager I'll call Chris. As he was serving the customer in front of me, the store phone started ringing, but he concentrated on helping his customer instead of answering it. After about a minute, the cashier in the next checkout stand turned around, gave him a look of unbridled hate, and bellowed, *"Chris, what is wrong with you? Can't you hear that thing? Pick it up!"* Chris turned bright red and looked as if he was going to cry. The woman in front of me looked him in the eye and said in a loud voice, "Chris, just ignore her; I think you are doing a great job." Chris looked massively relieved, and I could see him calm down.

Supportive colleagues, and thoughtful customers like

this one, can help buffer you against the stress of working with a slew of assholes. As Ruth did with her "Satan's Cesspool Strategy," such conversations can be especially constructive when victims exchange coping strategies that help them survive the onslaught of ogres. But talking with other people about your problems isn't a panacea; in fact, it can be a double-edged sword. Loraleigh Keashly and Steve Harvey conclude that initial studies have found that emotionally abused employees who seek emotional support from friends, family, coworkers, and supervisors enjoy only small positive effects on their mental health. Keashly and Harvey argue that social support has weak effects because victims mostly talk to people who don't have the power to stop the bullies and abusers.

Worse yet, I've found that conversations, gossip sessions, and even therapy sessions led by professionals sometimes do more harm than good. These gatherings sometimes degenerate into "bitch sessions" where victims complain bitterly about how bad things are and how powerless they are to stop it. I saw this happen at a hospital where external consultants were leading a series of workshops on job burnout. These poorly managed sessions started out with statistics about how badly nurses were abused by doctors and how many other sources of stress they faced—bad management decisions, difficult patients and families, and so on. This bad news sparked complaining and feelings of helplessness and hopelessness among the nurses, in large part because facilitators did not steer the conversation to ways these problems could be reframed or to strategies for gaining small wins—let alone to organizational strategies for implementing a no asshole rule.

I remember asking one nurse how the sessions were going, and she told me, "I walk into those sessions in a good mood, but always leave depressed. They are making me hate my job; all we do is bitch, bitch, bitch!" Remember that emotions are extremely contagious, so if you are going to create places, networks, and regular meetings to talk about how to cope with the assholes you work with, focus on ways to reframe events that reduce stress and on means for gaining small wins—not on creating arenas that produce and spread feelings of despair.

Fight and Win the Right Small Battles

Using a small-wins strategy can enhance your feelings of control, make things around you a little better, and maybe—just maybe—chip away at the vile and vicious culture in which you are trapped and start making it a bit better.

This approach requires constantly looking out for small but sweet victories that you can win, a tactic used by many of the more than 120 American workers interviewed in *Gig*, especially those who dealt with belligerent people. Some of these workers looked for moments when they could gently teach the angry people around them to calm down rather than escalate their anger. Prison guard Franklin Roberts said, when dealing with inmates, "I never yell at them. They get mad at me and yell their heads off. . . . They go wild. But you don't yell at them. You never want to lose face in front of these guys. If they start yelling, you start whispering. You just don't play their game." As Roberts pointed out, although inmates are dangerous and will still holler at you, by staying calm, a prison guard slowly gains their respect, reduces the risk he or she will be attacked, and gets hollered at and threatened less as a result.

Although most of us don't guard prisoners for a living, Roberts's method of relentlessly responding to irate people with calmness and respect can be used with assholes in any workplace. If, through one conversation at a time, you can teach them that you aren't going to catch their asshole poisoning, they may catch your calm and kindness and treat you with respect—even if they don't offer the same courtesy to others.

Gentle reeducation is a related strategy for small wins during interactions with assholes. The idea is to gently explain to your tormentor the demands you face or other reasons why you don't really deserve their wrath. *Gig* shows how Los Angeles bus driver Lupita Perez used this tactic to calm irate "civilians." Take the passenger who yelled at her, "You get paid to do nothing. You don't do nothing but drive." Perez calmly explained, "Not only do I have to take care of you and everyone else on the bus, but I have to take care of the bus, myself, people crossing the street, people driving their cars. . . . Madam, I'll gladly let you take this shift and, hey, I'll sit back there and relax for a while." The spiteful passenger apologized, and as Perez said, "I kind of opened her eyes." A small win like that not only gives the target of abuse a sense of control and makes things just a little better for a few minutes; if used consistently and skillfully over time, on one jerk after another, the series of small wins can chip away at the source of hostility—in this case, rude passengers.

De-escalation and reeducation are relatively low-risk strategies because, although they may fail, chances are low that such turn-the-other-cheek approaches will provoke jerks to crank up the wrath they are spewing out at you. Riskier small-wins strategies entail confronting an asshole head-on, exacting revenge, putting the asshole in his or her place, and "outing" and humiliating the jerk. Be warned, however, that such approaches are dangerous: aggression often provokes more aggression, so you risk sparking a vicious cycle of insults and personal attacks. And doing battle with a person who has greater power can be hazardous to your mental health and job security. Yet if you study your oppressor, pick the right moment, and are willing to take a chance, you might be rewarded with some meaningful little victories.

For starters, bide your time until just the right moment comes to pay back your local jerk for all the abuse you've endured, and exact some sweet revenge. My favorite payback story came from a producer of a Boston radio station, who was working with me to schedule a segment on "workplace weasels." She told me about the worst boss she ever had. The guy made "one hundred times more than I did" and was constantly "putting me down and vi-olating my personal space." In particular, her boss often ate her food, just walking up to her desk and eating part of her lunch or any snacks that she had. She felt invaded and ripped off, and even though she asked him to stop, he kept doing it. One day she made some chocolates out of Ex-Lax, the chocolate-flavored laxative, and left them out on her desk. Sure enough, her boss came by and de-voured them without asking permission. When she told him what was in them, "he was not happy." This act of re-venge is not only funny, it is inspired because she picked a way to get back at him when he had no rational de-fense. It was his just punishment for stealing her food, and he knew it.

Another revenge tactic was explained to me years ago by my friend Sue Schurman, who is now president of the National Labor College in Silver Spring, Maryland. Sue worked for several years as a bus driver in the 1970s in Ann Arbor, Michigan, where she eventually became a union leader. Even in a relatively small city like Ann Arbor, bus drivers constantly tangle with other drivers who are aggressive and sometimes hostile. Sue told me that when she took rookie drivers under her wing, one of the first things she taught them was that a skilled driver "never had an accident that is an accident," and instead, accidents should be "punishments" that bus drivers inten-tionally inflict on "crazy drivers." She went on to say that city bus drivers were permitted three accidents a year without facing disciplinary action, and that she advised new drivers to "save one for Christmas time, because that is when all the jerks are out, and you will want to get back at one of them."

Bus drivers work in settings where there are many hostile interactions with motorists, and drivers have limited control over their tormentors. Although they only occasionally exact revenge from the constant parade of jerks that they face, the *feeling* that they have the power to do it—the almighty perception of control—is essential for sustaining their mental health. Sue won numerous safety awards and had few accidents during the years she was a bus driver, but as she recently wrote to me, "The delicious thought that you could punish the assholes was an important psychological safety valve. The thought alone was sufficient to help you manage your anger."

The final tactic for battling back is even riskier then exacting revenge, but if it works, it is extremely effective: call their bluff. Some oppressors are all puffed up with tough talk, but after you watch them for a while, you may realize that they are sheep in wolves' clothing (much like some schoolyard bullies I faced in my youth). One *Harvard Business Review* reader described to me how she called a bully's bluff:

I do want to add that these bullies usually pick on those who will not stand up for themselves. I once worked for a social service organization that had a "major" bully . . . pun intended. He was a retired army major, and he had a knack for peeling the skin off those who showed any form of weakness, insecurity, or indecisiveness. He tried it on me a few times. One day, I'd had just enough aggravation that when he started on me, I just gave him a steely look and said that if he ever spoke to me that way again, I'd take him out at the knees, and that I was not paid to nor would I stand for any form of abuse, insults or shit from him ever again. I never had to again. He got the message.

This *HBR* reader had a lot of courage. A less risky strategy is to watch what happens when others get the courage to stand up to the local asshole. If, as in this case, the blowhard backs down, it means that your chances of a small win are higher—and if you and your oppressed colleagues gang up on the bully, he or she may change or, better yet, leave for good.

The Upshot: You Might Be Able to Take It, but Are You Really Trapped?

If you are stuck working with an asshole or, worse yet, hoards of them, there are ways to limit the damage. You can help protect your body and mind by reframing the abuse as something that isn't your fault and won't magically disappear—and by learning not to give a damn about those jerks and their vile organization. You might also look for small wins: seek and fight those little battles that you have a good chance of winning. Those modest victories will help you feel in control and just might help make things a bit better, and if you keep chipping away and others join your quest, things just might get a lot better for everyone in the long haul. I wrote this chapter because many people really are trapped with a bunch of assholes and, for financial or personal reasons, have no immediate escape route. And certainly, we all need to endure occasional encounters with assholes.

But there is a dark side to these ideas. They might provide just enough protection (or, worse yet, fuel just enough delusion of protection) to stop people from bailing out of relentlessly demeaning situations—even when they have exit options. I am, for example, disturbed by Jerrold's reports in *Gig* about the constant abuse that he took from Brad, the executive producer he fawned over. I worry that Jerrold's astounding hardiness and resilience sent the wrong message to Brad: that insulting and even assaulting his underlings was acceptable because he was such a rich and powerful person doing such important things. Jerrold joked that he will probably work for Brad until he has a nervous breakdown—a sad sentiment because it rings so true. The unfortunate implication is that if you are like Jerrold, and perhaps too skilled at lowering your expectations and taking comfort in the smallest of wins, it may keep you from escaping an abusive boss or organization.

On the other hand, perhaps Jerrold wouldn't mind catching asshole poisoning if it would help him become just as rich, powerful, and famous as his boss. I wish that being all asshole all the time was bad in every way—I detest them and am ashamed of (nearly all) the times that I've acted like one. Unfortunately, although assholes do far more harm than good, the next chapter shows that there is an upside to acting like an asshole.

CHAPTER 6

The Virtues of Assholes

I didn't want to write this chapter. But some of my closest and smartest friends kept arguing that it was a necessary evil. They convinced me that the book would be naive and incomplete if I didn't talk about the upside of acting like an asshole. And they kept raising compelling examples of people who seem to succeed *because* they are certified assholes.

Exhibit one was Steve Jobs, who is CEO of Apple, former CEO of Pixar, and the largest shareholder in Disney (after selling Pixar to Disney). It sometimes seems as if his full name is "Steve Jobs, that asshole." I put "Steve Jobs" and "asshole" in Google and got 89,400 matches. I asked some insiders to nominate the most (allegedly) demeaning leaders in entertainment and high technology to get some "comparison assholes," because Jobs's companies are in these industries. Michael Eisner, former Disney

CEO, was mentioned constantly, yet "Michael Eisner" and "asshole" produced a relatively paltry 11,100 Google hits. And in high technology, Oracle's infamously difficult "Larry Ellison" and "asshole" generated a mere 750 hits.

The scariest—and most entertaining—stories come directly from people who have worked for Jobs. *Wired* magazine summed up a reunion of 1,300 ex-Apple employees in 2003 by saying that even though Jobs didn't attend, he was the main topic of conversation, especially tales of his tirades and tantrums. In one attendee's words, "Everyone has their Steve-Jobs-the-asshole story." As a faculty member at the Stanford School of Engineering, which is in Apple's backyard, I've heard such stories over the years myself. Take the manager I spoke with (just days after it happened) about a tantrum that Jobs had at his now-defunct computer company NeXT. He told me that Jobs started screaming, crying, and making threats because the color of the new NeXT vans did not precisely match the shade of white that the manufacturing facility was painted. To appease Jobs, NeXT manufacturing managers had to spend precious hours (and thousands of dollars) getting the vans repainted in *exactly* the same shade.

Yet the people who tell these stories argue that he is among the most imaginative, decisive, and persuasive people they've ever met. They admit that he inspires astounding effort and creativity from his people. And all suggest—although his tantrums and nasty critiques have driven the people around him crazy and driven many away—they are a crucial part of his success, especially his pursuit of perfection and relentless desire to make beautiful things. Even those who despise him most ask me, "So, doesn't Jobs prove that some assholes are worth the trouble?"

For me, it wouldn't be worth the trouble to work with Jobs or someone like him. But I've become convinced that it's naive to assume that assholes *always* do more harm than good. So this chapter is devoted to the upside of assholes. Beware, however, that these ideas are volatile and dangerous: they provide the ammunition that deluded and destructive jerks can use to justify, and even glorify, their penchant for demeaning others.

The Virtues of Nastiness

GAINING PERSONAL POWER AND STATURE

Numerous studies show that we expect powerful people to spew out anger at powerless people, and there is also evidence that such nastiness can help people gain more influence over others. Even if we don't realize it, we expect powerful people to express pride and take credit when things go well, and to convey anger and blame toward underlings when things got wrong. People at the bottom of the pecking order struggle to maintain a toehold in their precarious positions by expressing warmth, flattery, deference, and, when things go wrong, apologies to higher-status members.

One reason that alpha males and females act like

bullies is we let them, and actually subtly encourage them to, get away with it. Studies by Stanford's Lara Tiedens and her colleagues suggest it is often a "kiss-up, slap-down world," and strategic use of anger and blame can help push yourself up the hierarchy and knock others down. Tiedens demonstrated this in an experiment in which, during U.S. Senate debates about whether Bill Clinton should be impeached, she showed recent film clips of the then-President. In one clip, Clinton expressed anger about the Monica Lewinsky sex scandal, and in the other, he expressed sadness. Subjects who viewed an angry Clinton were more likely to say he should be allowed to remain in office and not be severely punished, and that "the impeachment matter should be dropped"— in short, he should be allowed to keep his power. Tiedens concludes from this experiment, and from a host of related studies, that although angry people are seen as "unlikable and cold," strategic use of anger—outbursts, snarling expressions, staring straight ahead, and "strong hand gestures" like pointing and jabbing—"creates the impression that the expresser is competent."

More broadly, leadership research shows that subtle nasty moves like glaring and condescending comments, explicit moves like insults or put-downs, and even physical intimidation can be effective paths to power. Rod Kramer, another Stanford colleague, showed in *Harvard Business Review* how "intimidators" including former U.S. President Lyndon B. Johnson, former Hewlett-Packard CEO Carly Fiorina, former Miramax head Harvey Weinstein, former Disney CEO Michael Eisner, and, of course, Apple CEO Steve Jobs gained and expanded their power through the strategic use of nasty stares, put-downs, and bullying. Kramer explains how Johnson studied other people closely and used strategic insults and temper tantrums that were fine-tuned to play on the insecurities of fellow politicians. Kramer also reports that Fiorina was admired and feared for her ability to "stare down opponents."

Kramer's article "The Great Intimidators" portrays Hollywood's Harvey Weinstein as the definitive "rough, loud, in-your-face" intimidator, the master of using "contrived anger" to wield "porcupine power." A 2002 *New Yorker* story by Ken Auletta described the time that Weinstein was upset because rumors were flying that he had started a vicious whispering campaign to discredit *A Beautiful Mind*—a Universal Pictures film that was competing with his *In the Bedroom* for an Academy Award. Weinstein believed that Universal chair Stacey Snider was spreading these rumors about him. So Weinstein cornered Snider at a party and went on the attack. Auletta reported, "To the petite Snider, he was a fearsome sight—his eyes dark and glowering, his fleshy face unshaved, his belly jutting forward half a foot or so ahead of his body. He jabbed a finger at Snider's face and screamed, 'You're going to go down for this!'" Although Weinstein eventually apologized to Snider, Kramer asserts that such calculated sound and fury served Weinstein well throughout his Hollywood career, producing films that have garnered over 50 Academy Awards.

Kramer argues that these intimidators aren't really bullies because they use intimidation strategically rather than to just make themselves feel good. I disagree. If a person twice your size cornered you, screamed at you, and made threatening gestures, every "expert" I know would say you were bullied, and I'd say that you had encountered an asshole. No matter what you call such people, the ability to act like an intimidating jerk—or at least to endure the onslaught of fellow jerks—appears to be an essential survival skill in many corners of Hollywood.

Kramer focuses on the power of intimidation. But there is also evidence that being a nasty jerk can help you get ahead in another way: *by making you seem smarter than others.* Jeff Pfeffer and I saw this style of power grabbing in action a few years back when we studied a large financial institution where people seemed to get ahead for saying smart things rather than doing smart things. Putting down other people and their ideas—what they might call "destructive confrontation" at Intel—was part of the status game at the company. These attacks were often done in front of senior management, as junior executives used biting criticisms (which sometimes bordered on personal attacks) to move their targets down the pecking order and to move themselves up.

These nasty status games might be explained by research on the effect uncovered by Harvard's Teresa Amabile in her *Journal of Experimental Social Psychology* article

"Brilliant but Cruel." She did controlled experiments with book reviews; some reviews were nasty and others were nice. Amabile found that negative and unkind people were seen as less likable but more intelligent, competent, and expert than those who expressed the same messages in kinder and gentler ways.

INTIMIDATING AND VANQUISHING RIVALS

As Rod Kramer shows, threats and intimidation can be used for gaining and sustaining a position at the top of the heap. Just like those alpha male baboons—which glared at, bit, and pushed their fellow primates to maintain their standing—that were discussed in chapter 3, people bully others to gain and sustain status. The use and virtues of intimidation to gain power over rivals is most obvious when physical threats are routine practices. If you've seen *The Godfather* or *The Sopranos*, you've watched mob bosses and organizations sustain dominance through threats and violence. My father learned that these aren't just fictional stories when he and a business partner tried to go into the vending-machine business in Chicago during the early 1960s. They tried to place vending machines in bowling alleys, restaurants, and other places that dispensed candy and cigarettes. Vending machines were controlled by organized crime at the time, as it was a cash business that produced revenues that were difficult to trace. My father and his partner were warned that if they didn't get out of the business, they would be harmed. My dad went back to his old job delivering coffee. But his partner remained

defiant and insisted that he wasn't afraid of the mob—
until someone broke his legs and he decided that, after all,
it was a good idea to get out of the vending-machine
business.

Intimidation is also part of the game in sports, especially in football, boxing, and rugby, where winning entails gaining physical dominance over your opponents.
But it also helps people succeed in sports where physical
domination is less explicit, such as baseball. The great
Hall of Fame outfielder Ty Cobb was perhaps most famous for bullying his way to dominance. Ernest Heming-
way put it harshly but fairly: "Ty Cobb, the greatest of all
ballplayers—and an absolute shit." He played from 1904
to 1928 and had more than four thousand hits and a life-
time batting average of .367. Cobb was infamous for hurt-
ing opponents and getting in fights with teammates,
opponents, and virtually anyone else he encountered on
and off the field. Biographer Al Stump described Cobb's
interpretation of the base-running rules as "Give me room
or get hurt." Stump explained what this interpretation
meant for a player named Bill Barbeau who tried to stop
Cobb from sliding into second base: "A hurtling body,
spikes extended, had hit Barbeau at the knees, sending
him backward, stunned. Torn from his grip, the ball had
rolled into the outfield. Cobb was safe. Barbeau's leg had
been cut, and the game-winning run had scored."

Of course, most people don't work for the mob or as
professional athletes. But many of us do work in the corporate world and have to deal with intimidating people.

Steve Jobs is, once again, the master. Andy Hertzfeld, a core member of the original Macintosh design team, recounted a message that Jobs left for Adam Osborne, the CEO of rival Osborne Computer Corp. in 1981. As Hertzfeld reported in his book *Revolution in the Valley*:

> "Hi, this is Steve Jobs. I'd like to speak with Adam Osborne."
>
> The secretary informed Steve that Mr. Osborne was not available and would not be back in the office until tomorrow morning. She asked Steve if he would like to leave a message.
>
> "Yes," Steve replied. He paused for a second. "Here's my message. Tell Adam he's an asshole."
>
> There was a long delay, as the secretary tried to figure out how to respond. Steve continued, "One more thing. I hear that Adam's curious about the Macintosh. Tell him that the Macintosh is so good that he's probably going to buy a few for his children even though it put his company out of business!"

Jobs's prediction came true. Osborne Computer was shuttered a couple of years later.

MOTIVATING FEAR-DRIVEN PERFORMANCE AND PERFECTIONISM

Fear can be a powerful motivator, driving people to avoid the sting of punishment and public humiliation. A huge body of psychological research shows that rewards are more effective motivators than punishments, and there is substantial evidence that people and teams learn and perform much more effectively when their workplace isn't riddled with fear. Yet there is also psychological research going back at least to famous psychologist B.F. Skinner that, although less effective than rewards, people will work to avoid punishment. And famous sociologists including Erving Goffman have also shown that people will go to great lengths to avoid public embarrassment.

Numerous famous leaders have instilled the fear of punishment, scorn, and humiliation in their subordinates, and apparently have used it to good effect. Rod Kramer described how the famously tough U.S. Army General George S. Patton used to practice his scowling "general's face" in front of the mirror because "he wanted it to be as terrifying and menacing a countenance as he could possibly make it." Patton's soldiers feared his wrath, but also fought hard for him because they admired his courage and did not want to let him down. Kramer also reports that Nobel Prize winner James Watson (who discovered the structure of DNA with Francis Crick) "radiated contempt in all directions," often "shunned ordinary courtesy and polite conversation," and could be "brutal." Watson intimidated his scientific rivals, whom he saw as unimaginative "stamp collectors," but inspired many of his students to become famous scientists because—as one put it—he "always introduced the right mixture of fear and paranoia so [that] we worked our asses off."

Leaders, politicians, and scientists who are effective

assholes are rarely nasty all the time; their followers are driven by both the "sticks" of punishment and humiliation and the "carrots" of hard-won warmth and recognition. I've already documented Bob Knight's history of outbursts, but he was also routinely warm and encouraging to his players as well. The well-documented psychological "contrast effect" helps explains why leaders such as Knight who have a history of demeaning and belittling their underlings—punctuated by warmth and praise—can generate much effort and loyalty.

Related research on "good cop, bad cop" effects shows that criminals are more likely to confess their crimes and debtors are more likely to pay their bills when they are exposed to both a nice and a nasty "influence agent," or a single person who alternates between being nasty and nice. The contrast makes the threat of the bad cop seem more menacing (and thus the punishment and humiliation more pronounced) and the good cop seem warmer and more reasonable (and thus someone worth pleasing) than when just a good cop or bad cop is encountered. In much the same way, the motivational effects of Knight's nastiness and niceness on his players were likely magnified, driving them to do everything in their power to avoid his painful wrath and to bask in his sweet praise. Kramer concludes that a similar motivation drives people who work with Steve Jobs to come as close to perfection as they can: Jobs both conveys massive confidence in his people (and himself) and expresses massive unhappiness when they fail. As one former Pixar employee put it, "You just

dreaded letting him down. He believed in you so strongly
that the thought of disappointing him just killed you."

BRINGING UNFAIR, CLUELESS, AND LAZY PEOPLE
TO THEIR SENSES

Unfortunately, even if you aren't a certified asshole,
and even if you despise people who deserve the label and
avoid them like the plague, there are times when it is useful to play the part of a temporary asshole to get something that you need or deserve. Polite people who never
complain or argue are delightful to be around, but these
doormats are often victims of nasty, indifferent, or greedy
people. There is much evidence that the squeaky wheel
does get the grease.

To illustrate, if you don't complain to your health in-
surance company when they initially decline to pay a
medical bill, the odds are virtually zero that they will reverse the decision and send you a check later. But complaining apparently pays off. A recent study by
researchers at the RAND Corporation and Harvard University found that of 405 appeals by patients to U.S. in-
surance companies that denied payment for emergency
room visits, 90% were eventually paid, for an average
payout of about $1,100.

Certainly, for both your own mental health and the
mental health of your targets, all complaints and other efforts to get what you deserve and to bring people to their
senses ought to be made, for starters, in a polite way. But

there are times when getting nasty, even having a strategic temper tantrum, seems to be the only method that gets through to people. In the 1990s, I studied telephone bill collectors. I spent hours listening in on their collection calls, went through a week of training, and spent about twenty hours making my own collection calls to people who were late with their Visa and MasterCard payments.

In the collection organization I studied, we were taught that there was no reason to "slam" hostile debtors, as they were already upset enough. The challenge was to calm them down and to turn their focus to paying the bill. In contrast, we were taught to "slam" debtors who seemed too calm or indifferent about their late bills. Skilled collectors used a harsh and tense tone with debtors who didn't seem "worried enough" about their overdue bills; the collectors made (legitimate) threats like, "Do you ever want to buy a house? Do you ever want to buy a car? If you do, you better pay up right now." The best bill collectors were nasty to the nice, relaxed, or seemingly indifferent debtors—because it helped create a sense of "alarm" and a "feeling of urgency."

There are also times when people are so clueless, incompetent, or both that the only way to create sufficient alarm is to throw a strategic temper tantrum. Even those of us who don't consider the temper tantrum a core occupational skill sometimes pitch a fit when nothing else is working. Consider an experience that my family and I had with Air France in the summer of 2005 when we were traveling home from Florence, Italy, and had a stopover in

Paris. When we arrived at the airport in Florence, the Air France agent told us that she could not give us boarding passes for our Paris–San Francisco leg (we were later told by another Air France employee that she could have, but was "probably just too lazy"). Our flight to Paris was so late that we had less than thirty minutes to make the long trek through the massive airport, make it through multiple security checkpoints, and get five boarding passes.

We made it to the transfer desk with about fifteen minutes to go. There were perhaps eight employees behind the desk; there was no line, only employees talking to one another. After spending several minutes politely trying to get them to pay attention to our plight, I turned to my wife and kids and said, "I have to start yelling at them; I have no choice, and I will stop as soon as they start helping." So I just started hollering about how late we were, how badly we had already been treated, and that they needed to help us *right now*. I was really loud and nasty. When they actually started paying attention to the problem, they realized how late we were and started scrambling. As soon as they started helping, I shut up, backed away from the counter, and apologized to my kids—explaining to them again that it was a strategic temper tantrum. My calm, nice, and rational wife then dealt with them (so there was a bit of good cop, bad cop, too). They produced the boarding passes quickly, pointed at the gate, and said, "Run as fast as you can, and you might make it." We barely made it, but we did make it.

In looking back at that experience, I really have no

idea what else I could have done to get those indifferent and clueless Air France employees to pay attention to our plight—they were treating us as if we were completely invisible until I started hollering.

The Upshot: Some Virtues Are Real, But Many Are Dangerous Delusions

The unfortunate truth is that, yes, there are occasional advantages to acting like an asshole. Unleashing your inner jerk can help you gain power, vanquish rivals, motivate fear-fueled performance, and bring clueless and incompetent people to their senses. And, yes, returning the favor to another asshole can feel good and even enhance your mental health.

There are other upsides, too. Another justification for acting like an asshole is that if you want to be left alone, either because you have work to do or are just sick of dealing with other people, glaring, growling, and other forms of grumpiness are splendid means for chasing unwanted intruders away. Over the years, I've noticed that Stanford faculty members who snarl at visitors seem to have no trouble working without interruption in their offices, while those who greet every unscheduled visitor with a smile seem to face a constant flow of students, staff members, and colleagues. The "good cop, bad cop" technique works here as well. Years ago, I had a coauthor who routinely crossed her arms and openly glared at visitors who knocked on my office door while we were working. Those visitors quickly got the message from my coauthor, and they didn't stick around very long after getting such treatment; indeed, they rarely knocked again. The result was that her hostile actions allowed me to be seen as a nice guy by all those visitors and still get the work done!

I've distilled the main lessons from this chapter into a short list; if you want to be the best asshole that you can possibly be for yourself and your organization, see "Do You Want to Be an Effective Asshole?" But I should warn you, as I did at the outset, that the ideas in this chapter are inherently dangerous. People who are destructive jerks can use these alleged virtues to justify and glorify their wicked ways. The weight of the evidence (see chapter 2) shows that assholes, especially certified assholes, do far more harm than good.

DO YOU WANT TO BE AN EFFECTIVE ASSHOLE?

Key Lessons

1. **Expressing anger, even nastiness, can be an effective method for grabbing and keeping power.** Climb to the top of the heap by elbowing your colleagues out of the way through expressing anger rather than sadness or perfecting a "general's face" like George S. Patton.

2. **Nastiness and intimidation are especially effective**

for vanquishing competitors. Follow in the footsteps of baseball legend Ty Cobb, and succeed by snarling at, bullying, putting down, threatening, and psyching out your opponents.

3. **If you demean your people to motivate them, alternate it with (at least occasional) encouragement and praise.** Alternate the carrot and the stick; the contrast between the two makes your wrath seem harsher and your occasional kindnesses seem even sweeter.

4. **Create a "toxic tandem."** If you are nasty, team up with someone who can calm people down, clean up your mess, and extract favors and extra work from people because they are so grateful to the "good cop." If you are "too nice," you might "rent a jerk," perhaps a consultant, a manager from a temporary staffing firm, or a lawyer.

5. **Being all asshole, all the time, won't work.** Effective assholes have the ability to release their venom at just the right moment and turn it off when just enough destruction or humiliation has been inflicted on their victim.

Sure, there are successful assholes out there, but you don't have to act like a jerk to have a successful career or lead a successful organization. There are lots of warm and caring people to demonstrate this point. I think of successful business leaders like A.G. Lafley of Procter & Gamble, John Chambers of Cisco, Richard Branson of Virgin, and Anne Mulcahy of Xerox. I think of Oprah Winfrey and one of the most thoughtful and polite superstars of all time,

Elvis Presley. It is also worth noting that many reputed corporate bullies have lost their jobs in recent years, at least in part because of their demeaning ways. Examples include Disney's Michael Eisner, Warnaco's Linda Wachner, and Sunbeam's Al Dunlap.

More generally, organizations that drive in compassion and drive out fear attract superior talent, have lower turnover costs, share ideas more freely, have less dysfunctional internal competition, and trump the external competition. It turns out that companies can gain a competitive advantage by giving their people personal respect, training them to be effective and humane managers, allowing them time and resources to take care of themselves and their families, using layoffs as a last resort, and making it safe to express concerns, try new things, and talk openly about failures. Being on *Fortune* magazine's list of "100 Best Companies to Work For" is linked to superior financial performance, and the evidence for the long-term financial benefits of treating people with dignity and respect—rather than treating business as a "race to the bottom line"—is documented in numerous studies by renowned researchers including Rutgers's Mark Huselid and Stanford's Charles O'Reilly III and Jeff Pfeffer.

This raises a difficult question: why do so many people act like assholes and believe it is generally effective even though there is so much evidence that it is a downright stupid way to act? My hunch is that many assholes are blinded by several intertwined features of human judgment and organizational life. If you are concerned that you or someone else you know is suffering from such delusions of effectiveness, check my list of "Why Assholes Fool Themselves," which is derived mostly from three major blind spots.

The first blind spot is that although most jerks succeed despite rather than because of their vile ways, they erroneously conclude that their nastiness is crucial to their success. One reason this happens, as much psychological research shows, is that most people look for and remember facts that confirm their biases, while they simultaneously avoid and forget facts that contradict their dearly held beliefs. Professional ice hockey provides an interesting example. People involved in the sport widely believe that the more a team fights, the more games it will win because opponents will be physically and psychologically intimidated. Yet a study of more than four thousand National Hockey League games played between 1987 and 1992 shows that the more fights teams were in (measured by fighting penalties), the more games they lost. Fighting may still help teams in other ways because, as Don Cherry (the most famous hockey announcer in Canada) told the *New York Times*, "The players like to do it, the fans like it, [and] the coaches like it." The best evidence suggests, however, that less fighting means more wins, even if most people involved in the game don't believe it.

The second blind spot arises because people confuse the tactics that helped them gain power with the tactics that are best for leading a team or company. As we've seen, there is evidence that—especially in places with nasty and competitive cultures—intimidating and putting down others can help people gain power. The rub is that team and organizational effectiveness depends on gaining trust and cooperation from insiders and outsiders. When leaders demean their underlings and treat partners from other companies, suppliers, or customers as enemies rather than valued friends, their organizations suffer. Mean-spirited backstabbers sometimes elbow their way into powerful positions and use their demeaning moves to protect their power. But unless they change their destructive ways and reputations as fearmongers, they will have a hard time gaining the trust and cooperation required for fueling top team and organizational performance.

The third blind spot stems from defensive measures that experienced victims use to protect themselves from cruel and vindictive actions, measures that have the side effect of shielding assholes from realizing the damage they inflict. For starters, victims learn to avoid their oppressor's wrath by reporting only good news and remaining silent about, and even hiding, bad news. This tends to feed an asshole's delusions of effectiveness. People also learn to "put on a show" when the bully is monitoring their actions. They dramatically change what they do when the boss or another powerful person watches them work, but once the jerk departs, they revert to the "wrong" things. So oppressors travel through life believing that they are inspiring effective action when, in fact, it only happens during the rare moments they actively impose themselves on underlings. People who are experienced at "asshole boss management" also learn that their survival depends on protecting themselves from blame, humiliation, and recrimination rather than doing what is best for their organization.

Outsiders learn how to survive, and even thrive, when jerks rule the roost as well. "Asshole taxes" are a good example: I've talked to several management consultants, plus a few computer repair technicians and plumbers, who quote premium rates to nasty clients—who often don't realize this is happening. These "asshole taxes" have two effects: one is to drive away nasty clients, and the other is that if the client does pay, say, twice your usual rate, you can justify it to yourself by saying, "They might be assholes, but I am punishing them for that and benefiting to boot." And once again, the jerks pay a penalty—either by being unable to attract the best people or by paying more for their services—even if they aren't aware of the self-inflicted damage.

Assholes also often don't realize that every time they demean someone—say, with a nasty glare, a mean-spirited joke or tease, treating a person as if he or she were invisible, or exaggerating their self-importance yet one more time—their list of enemies grows longer day after day. Fear compels most of their enemies to stay silent, at least for a while. But as their enemies' number and power grows, the enemies can lie in wait until something happens to weaken the bully's position, such as organizational performance problems or a small scandal. Then they pounce. It is impossible to be in a position of power without annoying and alienating some people, but seemingly cold, unpleasant, and unkind people often create more enemies than they realize.

WHY ASSHOLES FOOL THEMSELVES

Are You Suffering from Delusions of Effectiveness?

1. You and your organization are effective *despite* rather than *because* you are a demeaning jerk. You make the mistake of attributing success to the virtues of your nasty ways, even though your demeaning actions actually undermine performance.
2. You mistake your successful power grab for organizational success. The skills that get you a powerful job are different—often the opposite—from the skills needed to do the job well.
3. The news is bad, but people only tell you good news. The "shoot the messenger" problem means that people are afraid to give you bad news, because you will blame and humiliate them. So you think things are going great, even though problems abound.
4. People put on an act when you are around. Fear causes people to do the "right" things when you are watching them. As soon as you leave, they revert to less effective or downright destructive behavior—which you don't see.
5. People work to avoid your wrath rather than to do what is best for the organization. The only employees who

can survive your management style devote all their energy to avoiding blame rather than fixing problems.

6. You are being charged "asshole taxes" but don't know it. You are such a jerk that people are willing to work for you and your company only if you pay them premium rates.

7. Your enemies are silent (for now), but the list keeps growing. Your demeaning actions mean that day after day, you turn more people against you, and you don't realize it. Your enemies don't have the power to trash you right now, but are laying in wait to drive you out.

In closing, I want to make my personal beliefs crystal clear. Even if there were no performance advantages to barring, expelling, and reforming nasty and demeaning people, I'd still want organizations to enforce the no asshole rule. This book isn't simply meant to be an objective summary of theory and research about the ways that assholes undermine organizational effectiveness. I wrote it because my life and the lives of the people I care about are too short and too precious to spend our days surrounded by jerks.

And despite my failures in this regard, I feel obligated to avoid inflicting my inner jerk on others. I wonder why so many assholes completely miss the fact that all we have on this earth are the days of our lives, and for many of us, huge portions of our lives are spent doing our jobs, interacting with other people. Steve Jobs is famous for saying that "the journey is the reward," but for my tastes, as much as I admire his accomplishments, it appears that he has missed the point. We all die in the end, and despite whatever "rational" virtues assholes may enjoy, I prefer to avoid spending my days working with mean-spirited jerks and will continue to question why so many of us tolerate, justify, and glorify so much demeaning behavior from so many people.

CHAPTER 7

The No Asshole Rule as a
Way of Life

The first time that I ever heard about a book on assholes was more than thirty years ago. It happened at an Italian restaurant in San Francisco called Little Joe's, where customers sat behind a long counter that faced an open kitchen. Most of us came to see the flamboyant chef, who sang, joked with customers and employees, and entertained us by igniting dramatic flames with olive oil as he cooked. Employees wore T-shirts that said "Rain or shine, there is always a line," and waiting for a seat was good fun because of the constant banter and clowning around. One day, I waited behind an especially rude customer who was sitting at the counter. He made crude comments, tried to grab the waitress, complained about how his veal parmigiana tasted, and insulted customers who told him to pipe down.

This creep kept spewing his venom until a fellow customer approached him and asked (in a loud voice), "You are just an amazing person. I've been looking everywhere for a person like you. I love how you act. Can you give me your name?" He looked flustered for a moment, but then seemed flattered, offered thanks for the compliment, and provided his name.

Without missing a beat, his questioner wrote it down and said, "Thanks. I appreciate it. You see, I am writing a book on assholes . . . and you are absolutely perfect for chapter 13." The entire place roared, and the asshole looked humiliated, shut his trap, and soon slithered out—and the waitress beamed with delight.

This story is more than a sweet and funny memory. That incident at Little Joe's reflects seven key lessons about the no asshole rule that run through this book.

1. A few demeaning creeps can overwhelm the warm feelings generated by hoards of civilized people.

The abuse spewed out by just one jerk was ruining the experience for everyone at Little Joe's that day. Remember that if you want to enforce the no asshole rule in your organization, you'll get more bang for your buck by eliminating those folks who bring people down. Bear in mind that *negative interactions have five times the effect on mood than positive interactions*—it takes a lot of good people to make up for the damage done by just a few demeaning jerks. If you want a civilized workplace, take some inspiration from the CEO who made up the equivalent of twenty-five "asshole wanted posters" and then purged those assholes from the company. So the first things that you need to do are screen out, reform, and expel all the assholes in your workplace. It will then become easier to focus on helping people become warmer and more supportive.

2. Talking about the rule is nice, but following up on it is what really matters.

Announcing a no jerks allowed rule, talking about being "warm and friendly," or displaying a "no bozos" poster is nice. But all those words are meaningless—or worse—if they don't truly guide people in changing their behavior. There were no rules posted at Little Joe's, but almost everyone in the restaurant understood that although the food was good, most customers went there to catch and add to the infectious good cheer. When that aspiring author humiliated the nasty customer, he was enforcing an unwritten rule: you had no business being at Little Joe's if you were spreading asshole poisoning, because it ruined the atmosphere for everyone else.

Talking about or posting the rule isn't necessary if people understand it and act on it. But if you can't enforce the rule, it is better to say nothing. Otherwise, your organization risks being seen as both nasty and hypocritical. Recall the fate of Holland & Knight, the law firm that bragged they had "made it a priority to weed out selfish, arrogant, and disrespectful attorneys" and that they would enforce a "no jerk rule." They faced bad press when insiders expressed "disgust" with the firm's hypocrisy because an attorney with an alleged history of sexual harassment was promoted to a senior management position.

3. The rule lives—or dies—in the little moments.

Having all the right business philosophies and management practices to support the no asshole rule is useless unless you treat the person *right in front of you, right now, in the right way.*

That customer who claimed to be writing a book on assholes took less than thirty seconds to deliver his beautiful insult. In that moment, he reinforced the unwritten rule that Little Joe's was a place where employees and customers came to have fun, to laugh, and to joke, not to abuse and demean. The same lesson emerged from the most extensive "asshole management intervention" that I know of in American history, which involved more than seven thousand people at eleven different Veterans Administration facilities. Of course, the people at the VA used much more polite language—words like *stress, aggression,* and *bullying.* But I call it an asshole management intervention because the VA teams taught people how to reflect on and to change the little nasty things that they did, like glaring at people and treating them as if they were invisible.

In other words, they helped assholes recognize how and when they did their dirty work—and they showed them how to change such destructive behavior.

4. Should you keep a few assholes around?

The incident at Little Joe's shows that very bad people can be a very good thing—if they are handled right. That flaming asshole was perfect for chapter 13 because his antics showed every customer and employee in that crowded place how *not* to behave at that place. But I want to warn you that allowing a few creeps to make themselves at home in your company is dangerous. The truth is that assholes breed like rabbits. Their poison quickly infects others; even worse, if you let them make hiring decisions, they will start cloning themselves. Once people believe that they can get away with treating others with contempt or, worse yet, believe they will be praised and rewarded for it, a reign of psychological terror can spread throughout your organization that is damn hard to stop.

5. Enforcing the no asshole rule isn't just management's job.

Keep in mind that the aspiring author at Little Joe's wasn't a manager. He wasn't even an employee. He was just a customer waiting in line.

The lesson is that the no asshole rule works best when everyone involved in the organization steps in to enforce it when necessary. Just think of the simple math. If, say, you work in a store that has one manager, twenty-two employees, and several hundred customers, it is impossible to expect that one manager to be everywhere at once, enforcing the no asshole rule or, for that matter, any other norm about how people are expected to act in the organization.

But if every employee and customer, as well as the manager, understands, accepts, and has the power to support the rule, then it is a lot harder for any given customer to get away with being a flaming asshole.

Treating people right means conveying respect, warmth, and kindness to them—and assuming the best about their intentions. But the game changes when people demonstrate that they are unmitigated jerks. And it is a lot easier to enforce the rule when everyone feels obligated to let bullies know that their nastiness is ruining the joy for everyone else and—as that clever customer did by embarrassing that flaming asshole—when everyone takes responsibility for pressing the "delete button" to expel assholes from the system.

6. Embarrassment and pride are powerful motivators.

That abusive customer at Little Joe's was stopped in his tracks because he was embarrassed. I can still remember how his face turned bright red, how he turned silent and stared ahead as he finished his meal, and how he avoided eye contact with people standing in line as he headed out. As renowned sociologists like Erving Goffman have shown, human beings will go extreme lengths to save face, to feel respected, and to avoid embarrassment and feelings of shame.

This simple insight highlights and glues together much of the advice in this book. In organizations where the no asshole rule reigns, people who follow it and don't let others break that rule are rewarded with respect and appreciation. When people violate the rule, they are confronted with painful, and often public, embarrassment and the feelings of shame that goes with it. True, it rarely happens as swiftly and thoroughly as it did that day at Little Joe's. At most places that enforce the rule, the delete button is powered with a more subtle blend of respect and humiliation. But it still happens.

7. Assholes are us.

I suspect that when you heard the Little Joe's story, you identified with the customers and employees who were offended by that jerk. And maybe—like me—you secretly dreamed that someday, just once, you could summon the spontaneous wit and courage to bring down an asshole just like that clever customer did.

But let's look at it another way. Think about the times when you were the guy at the counter, when you were the asshole in the story. I wish I could say I've never been that guy, but that would be a bold-faced lie, as I've confessed at several junctures in this book. If you want to build an asshole-free environment, you've got to start by looking in the mirror. When have you been an asshole? When have you caught and spread this contagious disease? What can you do, or what have you done, to keep your inner asshole from firing away at others?

The most powerful single step you can take is to follow "da Vinci's rule" and just stay away from nasty people and places. This means you must defy the temptation to work with a swarm of assholes, regardless of a job's other

perks and charms. It also means that if you make this mistake, get out as fast as you can. And remember, as my student Dave Sanford taught me, that admitting you're an
asshole is the first step.

The Upshot

The essence of this little book is pretty simple: We are all
given only so many hours here on earth. Wouldn't it be
wonderful if we could travel through our lives without en-
countering people who bring us down with their demeaning remarks and actions?

This book is aimed at weeding out those folks and at
teaching them when they have stripped others of their esteem and dignity. If you are truly tired of living in Jerk
City—if you don't want every day to feel like a walk down
Asshole Avenue—well, it's your job to help build and
shape a civilized workplace. Sure, you already know that.
But isn't it time to do something about it?

Dear Reader,

As you've seen in this book, I've learned a great deal from people who have sent me stories and suggestions about *The No Asshole Rule*. I'd love to keep it going. So if you would like to send me an e-mail about your experiences with assholes, what you've learned about taming them, how you endure them, or anything else, please visit my blog at www.bobsutton.net and just click on "Email Me" in the upper left corner. You can also read and comment on other stories of workplace assholes and their management, new articles and research on the workplace, and related opinions and news on my blog. Please note that by sending me your story, you are giving me permission to use it in the things that I write and say. But I promise not to use your name unless you give me explicit permission.

Thanks, and I look forward to hearing from you.

Robert Sutton
Stanford University

ADDITIONAL READING

Here are some of my favorite books and articles for those of you who want to learn more about nasty people, the damage they do, and how to stop them. Included are a few of my favorite books about famous jerks, as well as selections about people and their workplaces.

Ashforth, Blake. "Petty Tyranny in Organizations." *Human Relations* 47 (1994): 755–79.

Bowe, John, Marisa Bowe, and Sabin Streeter, eds. *Gig: Americans Talk About Their Jobs at the Turn of the Millennium.* New York: Crown, 2000.

Buchanan, Paul. "Is it Against the Law to Be a Jerk?" Essay for the Washington State Bar Association, http://www.wsba.org/media/publications/barnews/archives/2001/feb-01-against.htm, 2001.

Cowan, John. *Small Decencies: Reflections and Meditations on Being Human at Work.* New York: HarperBusiness, 1992.

Davenport, Noa, Ruth Distler Schwartz, and Gail Pursell

Elliott. *Mobbing: Emotional Abuse in the American Workplace.* Ames, Iowa: Civil Society Publishing, 2002.

Einarsen, Ståle, Helge Hoel, Dieter Zapf, and Cary L. Cooper. *Bullying and Emotional Abuse in the Workplace: International Perspectives in Research and Practice.* London: Taylor & Francis, 2003.

Feinstein, John. *A Season on the Brink: A Year with Bob Knight and the Indiana Hoosiers.* New York: Simon & Schuster, 1989.

Fox, Suzy, and Paul E. Spector, eds. *Counterproductive Work Behavior: Investigations of Actors and Targets.* Washington, D.C.: American Psychological Association, 2005.

Frost, Peter J. *Toxic Emotions at Work: How Compassionate Managers Handle Pain and Conflict.* Boston: Harvard Business School Press, 2003.

Hornstein, Harvey A. *Brutal Bosses and Their Prey: How to Identify and Overcome Abuse in the Workplace.* New York: Riverhead Press, 1996.

Huselid, Mark A., Brian E. Becker, and Richard W. Beatty. *The Workforce Scorecard: Managing Human Capital to Execute Strategy.* Boston: Harvard Business School Press, 2005.

Kramer, Roderick M. "The Great Intimidators." *Harvard Business Review,* February 2006, 88–97.

MacKenzie, Gordon. *Orbiting the Giant Hairball: A Corporate Fool's Guide to Surviving with Grace.* New York: Viking, 1998.

McLean, Bethany, and Peter Elkind. *The Smartest Guys in the Room: The Amazing Rise and Scandalous Fall of Enron.* New York: Portfolio, 2003.

Media.mit.edu/press/jerk-o-meter. Visit this site to learn more about how the Jerk-O-Meter works and the research that led to this invention.

Mnookin, Seth. *Hard News: The Scandals at* The New York Times *and Their Meaning for American Media*. New York: Random House, 2004.

O'Reilly, Charles A., and Jeffrey Pfeffer. *Hidden Value: How Great Companies Achieve Extraordinary Results with Ordinary People*. Boston: Harvard Business School Press, 2000.

Pearson, Christine M., and Christine L. Porath. "On the Nature, Consequences, and Remedies of Workplace Incivility: No Time for 'Nice'? Think Again." *Academy of Management Executive* 19, no. 1 (2005): 7–18.

Pfeffer, Jeffrey. *The Human Equation: Building Profits by Putting People First*. Boston: Harvard Business School Press, 1998.

Seligman, Martin. *Learned Optimism: How to Change Your Mind and Your Life*. New York: Free Press, 1998.

Stump, Al. *Cobb: A Biography*. Chapel Hill, N.C.: Algonquin, 1994.

Van Maanen, John. "The Asshole." In *Policing: A View from the Streets*, edited by P.K. Manning and John Van Maanen, 231–38. Santa Monica, Calif: Goodyear, 1978.

Weick, Karl. "Small Wins: Redefining the Scale of Social Problems." *American Psychologist* 39 (1984): 40–49.

ACKNOWLEDGMENTS

The No Asshole Rule was fun to write, which is something that I never thought I'd say about a book. This is my fourth management book. I love all of them, but I confess that there was a relentless ache that went with writing the prior three, which was largely absent this time. This was so much fun—despite the usual periods of frustration and confusion—because as soon as people heard the title, they started telling me great stories, pointing me to sources, and doing a host of other favors for me that made it the most delightful and energizing writing adventure of my life. It often seemed like I just had to listen to what people told me, remember some research and theory, look at what was happening around me, think about what had already happened, write it all down, and say a lot of "Thank yous" to everyone.

For starters, I thank the two editors who encouraged me to write the essays that led to this book. Even though I assumed they would clean up my language, or at least ask if such naughty language was really necessary, they never complained a bit about publishing the word *asshole* in their respectable publications. Senior editor Julia Kirby and editor Thomas Stewart of *Harvard Business Review* published "More Trouble Than They're Worth" in February 2004, and Ellen Pearlman, editor in chief of *CIO Insight*, published "Nasty People" in May 2004.

I am grateful to all of the people who told me stories, pointed me to evidence, and helped me in other ways. I can't use the names of many of them—to protect both the innocent and the guilty. But those I can thank include Sally Baron, Shona Brown, Dan Denison, Steve Dobberstein, Charlie Galunic, Liz Gerber, Bob Giampietro, Julian Gorodsky, Roderick Hare, Lisa Hellrich, "Susie Q" Hosking, Alex Kazaks, Loraleigh Keashly, David Kelley, Tom Kelley, John Kelly, George Kembel, Heleen Kist, Perry Klebahn, Randy Komisar, John Lilly, Garrett Loube, Ralph Maurer, Melinda McGee, Whitney Mortimer, Peter Nathan, Bruce Nichols, Nancy Nichols, Siobhán O'Mahony, Diego Rodriguez, Dave Sanford, James Scaringi, Jeremy Schoos, Sue Schurman, and Victor Seidel. I also want to give special thanks to my hero, the author Kurt Vonnegut, for sending me a handwritten postcard that gave me permission to reprint his poem "Joe Heller." I treasure it.

This book was also inspired by Stanford's department of industrial engineering and engineering management, of which I was part in the 1980s and 1990s (it was subsumed by Stanford's new department of management science & engineering in 1999). That was where I first saw the no asshole rule in action. I thank Jim Adams, Bob Carlson, Jim Jucker, and especially, department chair Warren Hausman for their grace and wisdom during those sweet years in that vigorous and charming place. I am also indebted to many other Stanford colleagues for the hundreds of big and small ways in which they have helped me, including Diane Bailey, Tom Byers, Kathy Eisenhardt, Deborah Gruenfeld, Pam Hinds, Rod Kramer, Maggie Neale, Charles O'Reilly III, Huggy Rao, and Tina Seelig. I want to single out several others for their astounding support. Steve Barley has encouraged me, put up with my quirks, and saved me from more assholes than I can count (including myself) over the years; he also taught me the virtues of the word *upshot*. Jeff Pfeffer is my closest colleague and friend at Stanford; he taught me how to write books and provides me with a constant stream of emotional support, ideas, and well-crafted nagging. I also thank James Plummer, the dean of the Stanford engineering school, and senior associate deans Laura Breyfogle and Channing Robertson, who are lovely people, each a model of compassionate and competent leadership. In fact, Channing used the "no jerks allowed" rule in a group that he led. Now that is my kind of dean! And an extra special thanks to Roz Morf, for caring so much and helping to make things easier in so many big and small ways.

I developed many of the ideas that led to this book when I served as a Fellow at the Center for Advanced Study in the Behavioral Sciences in the 2002–2003 academic year. This idyllic place is hidden away in a corner of the Stanford campus, which gives lucky scholars like me a supportive place to think, write, and get to know researchers from other disciplines. When I left the center in the summer of 2003, I was frustrated because I had started two books but had finished neither of them. Well, it took awhile, but now both *The No Asshole Rule* and *Hard Facts* are done, and neither would have had been written without the year I spent thinking about what they might be and trying to get them started. I especially thank Nancy Pinkerton, Julie Schumacher, and Bob Scott.

This book was also shepherded along by my literary agents, Don Lamm and Christy Fletcher from Fletcher & Parry. They caught and fueled my enthusiasm, helped me develop the proposal, and found the perfect editor. This brings me to Rick Wolff, my editor from Warner. I am mighty lucky to have worked with Rick because he "gets" this book so well. He understood from the first time we talked that beyond the bold title, crazy stories, and funny twists, *The No Asshole Rule* is about using sound evidence and management practices to tackle a problem that hurts millions of people every day.

I want to thank my family. My cousin Sheri Singer has encouraged me at every step and, as an experienced Hollywood producer, has taught me why Hollywood can be so nasty at times—even if oppression and bad will isn't really necessary for making movies and TV shows. I am indebted to my father, the late Lewis Sutton, and my mother, Annette Sutton. My father's work experience and advice taught me to avoid demeaning people, and my mother is more enthusiastic about this book than anything I've ever written. And without the help that Marijke and Peter Donat provided to take care of our son, Tyler, not only would this book never have been finished, I have no idea how our family would have made it through the last four years.

Finally, I am grateful to my sweet and practical wife, Marina, for her love and support during the thirty-plus years that we've been together. This little book is near and dear to Marina's heart, as it is about a problem that often plagues her profession. Marina has given constant advice, acted as a sounding board, read through the text, and made great suggestions. This book is dedicated to my sweet, smart, and funny children, Eve, Claire, and Tyler. My dearest wish is that you have long and happy lives that are free from entanglements with assholes.

INDEX